INSTRUCTIONAL MEDIA CENTER
William D. McIntyre Library
University of Wisconsin
Eau Claire, Wisconsin

D1777511

No Guarantees

No Guarantees

Chris Campbell

AN OPEN DOOR BOOK

New York

Maxwell Macmillan Canada
Toronto

Maxwell Macmillan International
New York   Oxford   Singapore   Sydney

Book design and production: Deborah Fillion

Copyright © 1993 by Chris Campbell

All rights reserved. No part of this book may be reproduced or transmitted in any form or by any means, electronic or mechanical, including photocopying, recording, or by any informational storage and retrieval system, without permission in writing from the publisher.

New Discovery Books
Macmillan Publishing Company
866 Third Avenue
New York, NY 10022

Maxwell Macmillan Canada, Inc.
1200 Eglinton Avenue East
Suite 200
Don Mills, Ontario M3C 3N1

Macmillan Publishing Company is part of the Maxwell Communication Group of Companies.

First edition

Printed in the United States of America

10   9   8   7   6   5   4   3   2   1

Library of Congress Cataloging-in-Publication Data

Campbell, Chris.
    No guarantees / Chris Campbell. — 1st ed.
      p.   cm. — (An Open door book)
    Summary: The author describes her addiction to drugs and alcohol, her denial of the problem, and finally her ability to deal with the reality of a situation that demanded help.
    ISBN 0-02-716445-4
    1. Campbell, Chris—Juvenile literature. 2. Narcotic addicts—United States—Biography—Juvenile literature. 3. Alcoholics—United States—Biography—Juvenile literature. I. Title. II. Series: Open door book.
HV5805.C35A35   1993
362.29'092—dc20   92-25183

▼

*Scott Jezierny and Sue Larracuente,
no matter how far the distance is
between us, you'll always be my best
friends. This book is dedicated to you
and all of our memories.*

▼

ACKNOWLEDGMENTS
▼

My parents, grandparents, and my family. I love you; thanks for your support.

Jenn Borg, you're like a sister to me. I love you. Be careful.

Everyone I was in group with at Foran: Jen K., Kathy D., Kelly D., Pete M., Rachel K., Maureen K., Chris K., Zeke, Kris M., Tara, Yvonne, Joe F., Cindy H., Cindy P., TJ, Dennis M., Chris J., Lynn A., Lisa P., Amy J., Nadine, Rob P., Chris S., Rick R., and Jason V.

Todd Jezierny, Ralph Mezzoni, Kelley Garland, Wade Jones, and Keri Smolinsky.

Sandy and Cindy Ambrose, thank you.

The Foran High School Student Assistance Team, especially A. Dodd, E. Brandon, and D. Ullman.

Ron Kosh, thanks for your support.

Dr. Robert Novelly, Pat McDonough, Chris Burke, and Greg Ryan. I'd be dead without you. This book's for you.

Bob R., I love you. Thanks for all your help.

Wakeman Hall and Arms Acres. Thanks to the patients and

the staff. Especially Harold, Ralph, and Gary.

Father Doherty, thank you, and may you rest in peace.

The J. A. Foran High School and Lauralton Hall classes of 1991.

From Foran: Margo Campbell, Sara Dodd, Don Feliciano, Jessica Gregory, John Hennessey, Mike Jacobsen, Erin Lippman, Darcy Richards, Peggy Sandor, and Grant Seelgen.

From Lauralton: Deirdre Foye, Jess Fuller, Joann Giambalvo, Brooke Gona, Jen Jensen, Karen Sapione, Julie Stewart, Laura Smith, Jen Suraci, Dianne Kan, Missy Link, and Amy Maxwell.

The Holm family. You're all very special to me. Thanks for everything.

Kathy Dougherty, Cindy Hudson, Kelly Donovan, Josh Pierce, Peter Milne, Jen Kelly, Rachel Kupson, Kenny, Mike, and Jay. What can I say? Thanks.

From ASU: my roommates Sybil Betsinger and Sarah Coburn. Also, Julie Reuvers, Jess Baker, Erin Alsop, Jes Palmeri, Jess Baumann, Staci Blanchard, Amy Sharman, Marvin Rosier, Jason, and Cube.

Stacey Hagreen. We think alike, and I hope that scares you. I'm very glad that we became friends.

CONTENTS
▼

- ▼ *Foreword* 11
- ▼ Chapter 1 13
- ▼ Chapter 2 17
- ▼ Chapter 3 31
- ▼ Chapter 4 39
- ▼ Chapter 5 65
- ▼ Chapter 6 91
- ▼ Chapter 7 97
- ▼ Chapter 8 107
- ▼ Chapter 9 135
- ▼ Chapter 10 169
- ▼ *Afterword* 189
- ▼ *Glossary* 191

FOREWORD
▼

This book explores a topic that may make some people uncomfortable—drug and alcohol addiction. Chemical dependency is something that almost everyone will have to deal with, in some way, during his and her life. It is a serious issue, and one that has changed my life immeasurably. I offer no solutions in this book, and I never preach about the wrongs of substance abuse. I can only share with you my experiences, and perhaps you will learn from my mistakes.

In writing these memories, I have two purposes. One is to sort out in my mind the events of my past and see how they have affected me. The other is to allow other people to learn from my experiences. I want people to realize how devastating drugs can be. The pain that I felt during the years that I actively used prompted this project. I believe that I have felt more than my fair share of pain and anger. I thought that drugs and alcohol were the answers to all of my problems. I avoided everything and I did all I could to not deal with reality.

Although my life is the focus of this book, obviously there are many other people who were affected by my addiction and recovery. My friends, family, teachers, and others all shared in my experiences. Throughout the book I have altered names to protect the identities of those who wish not to be recognized. In some cases I chose to condense the characteristics of people, making them into one person instead of many people with similar situations. Many other people in this book have chosen to allow the use of their names. The authenticity and reality of the story are unaltered.

CHAPTER ONE
▼

A large portion of my early memories is focused around drugs. Many of the adults I was in contact with as a child were involved in drugs. Most of my parents' serious drug use occurred before I hit my teens. It was more than my parents' use that I remember, though; it was several people's. In fact, I can probably think of more drug-related memories than any others. I believe that is what led to my addiction. I think that my addiction may have started long before my first drink or drug.

My fascination with drugs began early. I was obsessed with what the feeling of a high would be like, and how much it would change reality. It seemed normal to be involved with drugs. Using drugs was never far from my thoughts. I often daydreamed about them. But I never allowed myself to talk about these thoughts with anyone because I realized that most people did not approve of this behavior.

My dreams about drinking became a reality when I was seven years old. I swiped beers out of refrigerators, one at a time. I didn't do this very frequently, but often enough—

monthly at the very least. I didn't see anything wrong with what I did. I felt it was on the same level as taking a soda. I loved the taste of beer. I tried to get adults to let me drink from their beer cans as much as possible. I found it exciting, and I felt older. I thought I was more experienced than my friends.

It was in the third grade that my classmates and I started beating up on one another. I used to sit in the back of the room with these two boys, Joe and Chris. We'd beat each other all day. We used to see how many times we could hit one another's arms with a ruler before we bled. I gave most of that up in the next couple of years and started participating positively in my classes. In fourth grade I spent an hour and a half a week in front of my class, discussing with them some subject that I felt was important.

I was ten years old and in the fifth grade when I smoked pot for the first time. I liked pot a lot better than drinking because I found it much easier. Instead of drinking beer and feeling full or sick, all I had to do was smoke a joint. I loved it. I had a friend, Jen, who started smoking pot around the same time. She had two older sisters, and we amused them. They liked to get us baked. I started smoking pot and drinking on a regular basis. I said to myself, This is cool; I don't want to get into anything else. I'll just smoke pot and drink.

In the fifth grade I was admitted into my school's Academically Talented program for gifted students. I thought that I had the best of both worlds because I could be intelligent at school and then go home and escape from reality with the help of pot and alcohol. At home I didn't have to put up any fronts about who I was. At school, I thought I had to be different than I really felt I was. I hadn't discovered what sort of person I was yet.

At the same time I began to lose interest in regular classwork. I thought that I was too smart for regular school, and my lower grades reflected my boredom with my work. I got to be pretty pompous. But I was torn between wanting to do something that everyone was afraid to do—drugs—and wanting to be a successful student. My teacher had a habit of putting me on a pedestal in front of my class. I didn't want to be known that way. I wanted to be a rebel. So I went out of my way to prove I could get away with whatever I wanted to.

By the end of fifth grade I was building up a tolerance to alcohol and marijuana and I needed more to achieve the same effect I had had in the beginning. I was smoking pot at least twice a week, usually after school with Jen's sister Andrea.

During the summer before sixth grade, I got really drunk for the first time. It was the first time I ever threw up from drinking. That experience didn't turn me off drinking at all. I vowed to myself that it would never happen again. I planned to teach myself to hold my liquor no matter what.

By the time I hit sixth grade I felt it was my destiny to become an addict. That year I made a new best friend, Tricia. Tricia and I spent a great deal of time together with another kid in our class, Eric. Eric and I would drink vodka, shot for shot, after school at his house. His parents had no problem with us drinking or smoking pot at their house. They even stocked beer in the refrigerator for us. Eric was so uncontrollable that his parents didn't know what to do with him. I liked that.

Although I enjoyed getting high with my friends, I started using alone. I was tired of sharing my small amount of pot with other people. Eric was an exception. If I didn't have anything, Eric was always willing to give me some of his, and the same went for when I had pot and he didn't.

I wasn't a typical little girl. After first grade I never again wore a dress to any school function. I identified more with my boy friends than my girl friends. Even in kindergarten I remember being more comfortable with the boys. I wanted things like guns and war toys. I wanted to be respected and have people listen to me. That's what led me to people like Eric. He was obnoxious. Other kids never stood up to him. He showed me how to get what I wanted. No matter how much trouble I got into, Eric made it fun. When someone got into trouble, my teacher used to make them go into the back of the room and copy the dictionary. I had to do that many times. Eric would come back there and make me laugh. I lost all respect for school. I wasn't afraid of getting into trouble anymore.

There were a few good things I managed to accomplish, like dissecting two frogs and a fetal pig for the entire sixth-grade class. But overall I started getting into real trouble in the sixth grade. My whole class was made up of "troublemakers." Tricia, Eric, and I tormented our teacher relentlessly all year. She absolutely hated us. After our class graduated she transferred to be a fourth-grade teacher because she thought those kids would be less trouble. She was glad to see me go every Friday when I spent the day in gifted class.

I started smoking pot outside during recess. If Eric had spent our lunch money going in on a bottle, he and I would steal little kids' lunches. My teacher used to send kids out in the hall if they caused trouble. I was out there constantly. But since I was smart, I still got good comments on my report cards.

Toward the end of sixth grade I started really getting the attitude that I was superior to everyone else. The principal loved me. He was always telling me that I was the smartest kid in the school. That boosted my self-esteem, and I figured I could get away with whatever I wanted. During the last week of school I took a picture of one of my friends pulling his pants down. He got suspended, and the principal tried to get the pictures and the negatives. I wouldn't give them to him. That was just the beginning of my problems in school.

CHAPTER TWO
▼

The month before seventh grade I went to my first rock concert. My friend Jen and I were obsessed with Mötley Crüe, and since my mother was young, only 30, and liked the music, she took us. I smoked a joint in my backyard before we left, but I was more sober at that concert than at any I went to after that.

When middle school started I hated it. I was in the honors program and it was a relatively large class, about 30 kids. Suddenly I wasn't the only smart kid anymore. I couldn't stand the competition. So instead of working to keep up with everyone, I gave up. In class I was a real wise ass. My teachers couldn't stand me. I always had something to say. I got into an attitude of not caring about school or anything else. After the second quarter I got kicked out of the honors program. I couldn't maintain a B average.

I started smoking pot in school as often as possible. During class I'd get a pass to go to the band room to practice my trumpet and I'd smoke a joint in the bathroom before I got there. I also smoked pot during lunch and classes like sewing and cooking. Those classes were easy to get out of. It got to the point where I was afraid to face any class sober during school. I kept a bottle of Jack Daniel's in my locker throughout seventh and eighth grades. My teachers used to ask me why I asked to go to my locker so often. I wanted very badly to get into harder drugs such as cocaine.

The thing that really got me through middle school was that there were drugs everywhere. Tricia introduced me to many people that she'd met in her classes who also used during the school day. I smoked pot in the bathroom during class and lunch, and I smoked on the bus after school. Tricia and I drifted apart in school, but we remained friends. One day she introduced me to her 16-year-old friend Chuck. Shortly after we met he went away to try and stop using cocaine.

Around this time I met Zack. We met while I was at a friend's house. He was there talking to her brother. He heard us talking about pot and asked me if I was interested in trying cocaine. I said I was; I'd been waiting for an opportunity to do coke. Zack was 14 but he acted much older. We exchanged phone numbers, but I didn't think he'd really call me. He did, and eventually gave me my first gram of cocaine. A week after my 13th birthday I did my first lines of cocaine on his front porch.

In early June during seventh grade, Jen brought LSD to school and we decided to trip that day with her sister Andrea. Jen had done acid before, but it was my first time. I was nervous because I didn't know what to expect. At their house they gave me one hit. "One hit?" I asked. "I'll take three."

"This is acid," Jen explained, "and you haven't done it before. Only take one hit."

Andrea agreed with Jen. "LSD is nothing like anything else you've ever tried. Trust us."

I still insisted on having three hits. They frowned at me

but handed over the other two. The hits were tiny squares of paper with brightly colored bears on them, the dancing bears symbolic of the Grateful Dead. I stuck all three hits on my tongue and sucked on them. About ten seconds later I swallowed them. I was excited about my first trip. I didn't know it would end up being one of the worst drug experiences of my life.

At first I felt fine. The acid hadn't taken effect yet, and I thought tripping was fun. Then a wave of paranoia passed over me. I felt the need to get up and move around. I walked out onto the front porch, and Jen followed me. I looked all around for something to do.

Finally, I took a hammer out of a toolbox and walked out into the front yard, where I began banging on the metal garbage cans that lined the street. All of a sudden a black cat came running up to me. By then I was well into my trip, and I thought I saw trails flying behind the cat. Trails are streams of color that you think you see when you are tripping on acid. Because I was seeing trails, it looked to me like the cat was flying right at my face.

I threw my arms up in front of my face to stop the cat from attacking me. Even though it was nowhere near me, I was convinced that the cat was crawling on my body, and I swung the hammer wildly trying to knock it off. The whole time I was doing this, I was screaming that the cat was trying to kill me. Finally, I realized that the cat had run away and I calmed down a little.

Jen, Andrea, and I walked around West Haven for hours until my paranoia went away. At first, they were afraid to talk to me. We were all in shock over what the acid had done to me. Finally, Jen started laughing, and we all pretended that what had happened didn't bother any of us.

In June Chuck returned to Connecticut. He hadn't been using while he was gone but as soon as he got home he started again. At the same time, my relationship with my parents was deteriorating. There wasn't much communication among the three of us. My parents and I agreed that I was going through a stage of rebellion. I had no interest in my family. I was adjusting to middle school and I wanted to spend more time alone and with my friends. I was smoking pot every day. I was also using cocaine very frequently because Zack was getting into dealing more heavily. When I first met him, he sold only to people he knew, and only in small amounts. Now he was selling cocaine and crack 24 hours a day, to anyone who wanted it. He was supporting both our habits.

When I started the eighth grade, I made a terrible first impression on my teachers. I always had to talk back to them in class. I was obnoxious, never doing anything I was supposed to do. I talked to my friends with no regard for what was going on around me. I would sign out to go to the bathroom and not return for 20 minutes. I wasn't allowed to reenter the honors program. I still attended weekly gifted classes, but I was the only one who wasn't in honors, too. I felt like the other kids were smarter than I was, and that I didn't belong there. I asked my guidance counselor if I could leave the program. After analyzing my standardized-test scores and an IQ test I took, they told me I had an IQ of about 155. I was shocked. I knew I wasn't stupid, but I didn't think I was that smart, either.

I had my first blackout from drinking in October of that year. It was at a friend's birthday party. At school on Monday people were talking about things I did that I couldn't remember, like almost knocking out a girl and just being loud and rude. I found the experience both alarming and exciting. I felt I was finally living the life-style that I wanted. I was naive and unaware of the damage that could be caused by drugs and alcohol. I'd had an image of myself as a drug addict for some time, and it was appealing to me. The people I admired most at school were those who drank alcohol and smoked pot. I used to laugh at friends who voiced their concerns over my drinking and drugging. They told me it wasn't normal to use like I did. They said that 13-year-olds didn't do cocaine. I knew that *I* was too young to become an alcoholic. I didn't even have a real concept of what an addict was.

That winter I spent all of my free time getting cocaine. Zack was my major supplier. It wasn't very often that people at school would have a significant quantity of it. I thought I was in heaven because Zack never asked for anything in return. He was 15 and I was 13. He told me that he liked getting high with me and that he didn't mind giving me free coke. It was an unusual situation, definitely not normal. I was smoking at least two joints daily in order to ease my coke crashes. About three to five times a week, Zack and I drank together. Basically we stuck to beer and Jack Daniel's. I had my second blackout close to my 14th birthday. I heard that I almost passed out. People said I was a real jerk.

It was during eighth grade that I became very abusive, both physically and verbally. It was nothing for me to just walk up to someone I didn't like and punch them in the face. There was a kid in my class that used to piss me off a lot. He'd been in my class since fourth grade, and I was sick of him. So I started popping him in the face whenever I walked out of History. I told my teachers off at every opportunity. One time I actually hit one of my teachers, in the face, outside of school. I was at the peak of a cocaine high when it happened. I couldn't believe that I did it. He had no problem slamming my head into a wall. I don't blame him. I would've done the same thing.

I left class a lot. I was on the yearbook staff, and that took much of my time. There was also the American Industrial Arts Student Association (AIASA), band, and the school psychologist. Before I began seeing the school psychologist twice a week, I'd never gone to a therapist before. I enjoyed going, because I finally had someone to talk to about any subject that I wanted to talk about. The guidance department also got to know me quite well.

I was caught using many substances at school. I was found drinking, smoking pot, and snorting cocaine. I never got into trouble over it. I was very lucky, or so I thought. One time I was smoking a joint in the bathroom, and my English teacher came in to get me. She was too stupid to notice the scent of pot. I went up to one of my other teachers and said, "Look, the bitch didn't even realize I was smoking a joint in there."

He said, "I think you have a serious problem with drugs and alcohol."

I laughed. "I'm too young."

By the end of the year I would just break out a mirror and do lines on my desk. The people who sat around me in class thought I was crazy.

Since I worked in the school bookstore during lunch, I would get the keys and open it early. I was president of the Industrial Arts Club, so I basically did what I wanted because the club ran the bookstore. No one could get in there without me opening the door, except the adviser, but I could hear anybody putting the keys in the door. I did a lot of cocaine in there during lunch, either alone or with Eric. It was too risky to have anyone else in there. If we ever stopped being friends, they could turn me in.

Out of my five general teachers I had one favorite. I told him quite a bit about myself. I'd been feeling depressed since seventh grade, and I told him about my feelings of sadness. He eventually referred me to counseling because of a suicide gesture. I had slit my wrists with a razor blade. The cuts weren't deep, but the school seemed to think it was enough to warrant evaluating me. I had to talk to everyone—the nurse, my gifted-class teacher, the guidance counselors—but I didn't want to talk to them. Finally I hit it off with the school-system psychologist. I saw him every Monday and Wednesday, and occasionally Fridays. My parents knew about him because the school did an intervention. This is when the school feels a student is in danger and alerts the parents to the problem. My parents weren't crazy about the idea of me seeing someone, but he was a cool guy, so I went anyway. I had him come to the school once on an emergency call. I admitted to him that I thought I might have a problem with drugs. He said he already knew that. It was close to the end of the year, though, so all he could do was refer me to a private therapist. I never followed up on it.

One day at Tricia's house I thought I was going to die. I had snorted crystal meth and cocaine, and I was drinking as well. I was having severe chest pains, so I lay on the floor. I kept saying over and over, "What a rush!" Tricia's father saw me and was disgusted. Tricia ended up coming over to my house for a while, because I couldn't go over there high. In eighth grade no one was home in the afternoon but me. In previous years my mother had usually been home during the day, but in August 1986 she began working as an elevator constructor and didn't get home until late.

The spring of eighth grade was probably one of the worst times in my life. I not only snorted cocaine, I smoked it. I was also taking speed orally. Earlier in the year I had joked about suicide, but by this time I was serious. I made my first real suicide attempt in April. I was at a friend's house. They had a garage. Since we didn't have one, I saw an opportunity. I had carefully thought out all the methods of suicide, and carbon monoxide poisoning was a logical choice. My friend's father was out of town, and his car was in the garage. My friend and I were both high, and she gave me "permission" to kill myself. She was so stoned she had no idea what she was doing. As I was sitting in the idling car, I was happy because I thought the end was near. Then her older brother came in and yanked me out of the front seat. He screamed at me. I've never seen anyone so pissed before. There was nothing wrong with me physically, except dizziness and a headache.

That night I had a serious cocaine binge. The next day I was supposed to go to a state convention for AIASA. I'd entered a computer-aided drafting project in the competition, but I knew I wouldn't win and was too strung out to go. My adviser was disgusted with me.

The day after the convention, word got around school that I'd tried to kill myself. I was sent down to the nurse's office, where I was met by the school psychologist. I was telling him about the project I'd spent three months on, and how I was sure I didn't win. About ten minutes later my adviser showed up with my trophy. I'd won first place in the state in Computer-Aided Drafting (CAD) Level I, Mechanical. I couldn't believe it. He told me that my project was going on to the regional finals. If I won that, I'd be entered in the national competition. That news overwhelmed me, but it didn't negate dealing with the psychological evaluation the school was having done on me. My parents were called, and I knew they wouldn't be pleased. They weren't available to come get me, so my guidance counselor let me go home with a friend's father, who came and took us to his house. That felt strange, having other parents involved. When my parents came to pick me up, my mother said they were very disappointed. When I told them that I won the competition things eased up a little.

During the next three months I worked as hard as I could, between getting high and other activities, to prepare myself for the AIASA national finals. An architectural firm in Greenwich, a town about 45 minutes south of West Haven, volunteered its services to teach me to operate AutoCAD, the software package that would be used in the competition. They gave me two full-day classes and then lent me a computer, digitizer, and software to use at home. Another computer was donated for me to use at school. I was allowed to work on it whenever I felt like it. It seemed like I had immunity from everything. If I won at the national level, my school would win $20,000 worth of computer equipment, and so would I.

It was also around this time that I started getting more and more into speed. I thought it gave me energy to keep working toward the conference. I had a friend whose father was a doctor, and he got pills for his wife, who was a chronic dieter. They never noticed when I took handfuls at a time. I began using them three or four times a day. Sometimes I used crystal meth, a form of speed. Before gym I'd line it up on a mirror in the locker room for a group of us to snort in order to get more energy. That was when I decided to go to gym, which wasn't often. One day in homeroom I was shaking and had cold sweats from speed and cocaine. My homeroom teacher used to give me this pitying look that really bothered me.

I tried LSD again after that incident. This time I wanted to trip alone. My parents weren't home much that week because they were rescue workers where a building had collapsed. I decided to take advantage of their absence. I took the hits that I'd bought from Jen and went for a little walk on the beach. I must have sat on a bench looking at the water for at least two hours. The more I thought, the worse my depression became. I walked out onto a pier and I thought about suicide. I was becoming very self-destructive. Although it was low tide, I figured I'd die if I jumped from the pier. I was the only one there. I climbed onto the railing and jumped head first, falling on the rocks and then into the shallow water. It took me a few minutes to get up, because I'd almost knocked myself unconscious. My head was bleeding, but other than that I was okay. I walked home slowly and listened to my Doors tape until I felt more calm.

The next weekend was Memorial Day, and I was waiting for an article about me and the AIASA competition to be in the paper. The article appeared on the day I played trumpet in the Memorial Day parade. I felt great. I had finally accomplished something. I had high hopes for winning or at least placing in the national competition.

The article was good publicity for the school, and that meant a lot to the administrators because the school usually didn't get much good publicity. Everyone was very happy for me. When I screwed up, my teachers looked the other way.

One of my biggest problems was the lack of control I had over my anger. When I got angry, I lost it. It was June of eighth grade the first time I remember really losing control and going off on someone. I was in the bookstore with a girl that I really wasn't friends with anymore. At one time I had been friends with her, but our relationship had deteriorated rapidly because we had many conflicting views. She was strange, and didn't have many friends at all, mostly because suicide was the only thing she ever talked about. She came out and told me that she resented me for being president of AIASA because she had run against me and lost. She believed she deserved to be president more than me because she thought I was a loser. I couldn't have cared less if she was in AIASA or not. The only reason she wanted to be in it was that her only friend, Lisa, was in the club. She told me that. I was in the bookstore one day, setting up for lunch. She was in there, too, talking to Lisa. I had done some lines before they got there, so I was high. After trying to ignore her, because she was starting with me, I just snapped and punched her in the face. I think I broke her nose. Blood spurted all over the floor in front of her.

Instead of staying and making things worse, I left. The principal called me down to his office. After explaining my side of the story, he let me go, since I was going to Baton Rouge, Louisiana, to represent the school. The only thing that happened was that the girl's parents called me that night and threatened to have me arrested. But I told them that I would kill them all, and I never heard from them again.

I didn't go to my eighth grade graduation. That was the day I had to fly to Baton Rouge for the AIASA convention. I went to school for a half day to have people sign my yearbook. I ended up playing "Meet the Flintstones" on my trumpet in the hallway. The principal got a kick out of it.

My mother and I flew out to Louisiana without my father, because he was working on an important job. It was about ten hours before we actually arrived at our hotel. We only stayed there about 20 minutes. The place was crawling with roaches. Neither of us deal well with bugs, so I made it clear that I didn't care that it was midnight—there was no way I could sleep in a hotel that had roaches. Nothing bothers me like bugs. So we checked out and moved to a hotel across town, one that was bug-free. It wasn't a great start for the trip.

The national conference was an interesting experience. I decided that I wanted to go to Tulane University in New Orleans. That's how much I loved Louisiana. The day my event was scheduled we drove down to New Orleans for a few hours. It was great. Then we drove back for my event. It took four hours. It entailed making four diagrams on the computer, each a side of a given object. My adviser was there with me, but he wasn't allowed to give me any help with the drafting part of it. It was hard, especially since I'd never taken a class in drafting. During the break I called one of my friends. I was nervous. I didn't think I had done too badly when it was over. I thought I'd done pretty well. I'd worked out the drafting part the best I could.

Every day all of the participants in the conference got together for sessions. At one I had my first real experience of talking to a large group, an audience of 1,400. When someone made a motion to change the name of the organization I stood up, faced the group, and defended the old name. My adviser was very happy with me. Because of what I was like at school, he hadn't expected me to be so professional.

The night the awards were given out, I had to wait three hours before my event was announced. I came in fourth place out of fifteen contestants. I thought I was happy with that, but I wasn't. Since everyone at home had told me I'd win, I really thought that I would. After we left I was trying to keep myself from feeling disappointed, but my mother was pissed that everyone had psyched me up for success and I had lost. I started crying and told her I didn't need to hear that. I was disappointed enough at that point. I couldn't help but feel like I hadn't worked hard enough at the drafting.

Shortly after coming home from Louisiana I decided to attend a different high school than I'd planned. I wanted to start over and get a new identity. I picked Lauralton Hall, an all-girl Catholic school in Milford, a neighboring city. My mother had gone there for her freshman year.

My eighth grade graduation party was at my grandparents' house. I got drunk because there was a garbage pail full of beers. My friends and I just helped ourselves. We had fun.

Everyone was surprised that I was going to Lauralton because I wasn't the private-school type. My friends and I shared the theory that I might be able to get my act together by going to a new school, with people who didn't know about my past. We were wrong.

CHAPTER THREE
▼

At Lauralton I didn't want to have a reputation as a person who did drugs, but I couldn't seem to help it. I tried to keep it to myself, but that didn't change my attitude. I wanted to stop doing cocaine and speed. I thought that those were my only problems. I didn't want to stop drinking and smoking pot.

In October of my freshman year, I stopped using all forms of speed completely. It was extremely difficult to stop and I dealt with it by using cocaine more than I ever had before. I took the bus home with a girl that I had known in the middle-school gifted program. She was using at least as heavily as I was, if not more. Her name was Sarah, and we got to be better friends quickly. We did whatever we had to do to get high. If we couldn't do better, we would go to a drugstore after school and steal a box of Drixoral, an over-the-counter allergy medication. We'd take as many pills as we could. It was a down, and although I didn't like depressants, I did it anyway. I went to any lengths to get high.

Sarah and I wrote notes to each other in code. When we smoked pot during the day, we'd call it cookies. Like, I had cookies for lunch today. We had names for places we'd go to. There was one back door that faced the woods, and we called that Utah. That way, if someone got the note, they wouldn't find out what was going on.

I used a lot during the school day. It was easy. There were two bathrooms that were always empty. We would just crank the window open and smoke a joint. I did coke just about anywhere. I'd bust it out right on my desk, especially in French class. I sat in the back of the room, and my teacher always ignored me because of my disruptive sarcasm. Sarah and I talked about drugs constantly. Her boyfriend did a lot of coke, so she could get it when I couldn't. We met him at the bus stop once in a while during lunch or after school.

We almost got caught drinking in the basement of the school once. People were always bringing liquor to school in one form or another. I kept little bottles of vodka in my locker. One day I had a beer can right in my hand when the dean of students, an elderly nun, walked up. She didn't realize it was a beer, and she told me to make sure I threw it out when I was done. Food wasn't allowed down there.

At the end of October there was a sign on the bulletin board at school for a group called Sea Explorers. Sea Explorers is a division of the Boy Scouts of America, and members learn boating skills. Each group is called a Ship, and I joined Ship 25. My friend Karen saw it posted and she mentioned wanting to go. I thought it was a pretty funny idea, but it would be cool to go sailing during the summer. Our friends didn't think I would join. They didn't think I could stay in a group like that. I was nervous about going to my first meeting, but I needed to get involved in something. The first person I met was Wade. We ended up becoming really good friends, but I kept going to the meetings because of Al. It didn't take long at the first meeting I went to for us to realize that we both smoked pot. It's a strange thing about people who use. They can always pick out other people who use as well.

About two and a half months after I joined the ship we went on a camping trip to Camp Sequassen in Winsted, Connecticut. It was a three-day weekend, and together Al and I brought 11 joints. As soon as we arrived at the camp, we took off and baked it up in a lean-to. I loved it. We were stoned the whole trip. The first or second night we were there, we walked out onto the frozen lake to smoke. When we were walking back to the cabin, Al's best friend, Mark, started yelling, "pot heads!" across the field. I hadn't wanted anyone to know what was going on, but it wasn't hard for them to figure out. So everyone's first impression of me was as a pot head. I didn't care. I was getting high, and that was all that mattered.

About a month later the Ship had a fund-raiser at a local dance club on a Sunday afternoon. My friend Kate, from Lauralton, went to it with me. She wanted to get more involved in using. She hadn't really been exposed to drugs before meeting me. I was more than willing to share the world of drugs with her. We drank a couple of beers before going in. I don't dance, so I stayed at the table and rolled a joint in front of everyone. That was a real bright idea, especially since the skipper and his wife could have walked over at any time. Al and Mark took the joint into the boys' bathroom to smoke half. Then Kate and I smoked the rest in our bathroom. I thought that was what real fun was. I had forgotten what it was like to have fun without chemicals. At that club I was smoking cigarettes, too, which is no big deal, but it worsened the impression that Mr. Holm, the skipper, and his wife had of me. I thought that I was being good just waiting for the activity to end before I did any cocaine.

Shortly after the school year started I began selling drugs at school. I started out by selling joints, and then I chopped up aspirin and sold it to someone as cocaine. I only did that once. I knew people would catch on, even if they weren't familiar with the drug. Mostly I sold pills—muscle relaxants and other depressants. I got muscle relaxants by going to the emergency room and faking muscle spasms. It worked. Then one day I sold some to a girl I knew and warned her not to take the whole pill at once. But she did and passed out during class. She was taken to the hospital and was fine, but it scared me. That was the last time I took money for any drugs at school.

By this time I was still using cocaine almost daily. Once, when I rode to New Haven with my friend Will to buy some blow, he totaled his car on the way home. Luckily neither of us was hurt, but he was drunk and he knew there was no way he could avoid a DWI arrest. I couldn't deal with the police, who were sure to arrive soon, so he gave me the coke and told me to go to a pay phone and call Zack to come meet me. I sat on the sidewalk in front of the housing project I called him from. It felt like hours before he finally arrived. It was actually about 20 minutes. I didn't want to make it look too obvious, so every couple minutes I'd stick my nose into the bag and snort some coke. Will wasn't pissed, because the police searched him and the car on suspicion of possession, and we both would have been screwed if we had been caught. He was arrested for DWI.

At the end of my freshman year I was at the point where shooting drugs didn't bother me at all. I actually enjoyed needles. I started doing it with a 23-year-old guy, Joe. He and his roommate lived across the street from me. The first time I was real nervous about it. AIDS wasn't what scared me; the high scared me. I was afraid I would have a heart attack or something. After I was good and high from freebasing, Joe started playing the Grateful Dead. I was ready to try injecting coke. Playing Dead songs always got me in the mood to get high. So did Pink Floyd. Joe took the set he'd just used and rinsed it with water. Then he stuck it in my arm. It was the most intense high I'd ever felt. I loved it immediately. But I was afraid of getting track marks on my arm and becoming a "junkie."

It was then that I talked to Joe about my shooting heroin sometime. He laughed at me. He said that there was no way he was going to get a 15-year-old kid any heroin. It seems ironic to me now that he was willing to let me shoot coke with a dirty needle but he wouldn't get me heroin. I'm grateful that he didn't, though. I might be dead right now.

I thought that everything was going well for me. I wasn't one to brag about the drugs I did, but in my mind I still thought that I was better than most people. I laughed at the girls who got drunk off a beer or a wine cooler. I thought it was funny. The only thing I never told anyone was that I was shooting up. I was afraid to say it. When I said it, I sounded like an addict.

Just because we weren't going to the same school anymore didn't mean that Tricia and I stopped being friends. The only thing that put a strain on our friendship was her parents. Her parents were never very happy that she and I were friends. I always had the impression that they felt sorry for me, though, and I played on that a lot. More than once they told Tricia not to hang out with me. They thought I was a bad influence. Actually, Tricia was a pretty bad influence on me. I got high and drunk innumerable times at her house. So freshman year I gave her a key to my house so that she could stop by and get a drink or whatever on her way home from school. One day she stopped in when I wasn't home and ate a Valium that I'd left on the counter for later. Apparently she smoked a joint with her boyfriend, too. When she got home she was practically unconscious. Her father called from work and she could barely talk to him. He asked where she had gotten that way and, like an idiot, she said "Chris's house." That time her parents were really pissed. I didn't go over there for a couple months, and I didn't talk to her for a couple days. Her parents never acted the same toward me after that, I guess because I'd always been the troublemaker, not their daughter.

At the end of freshman year I wrote poems, to get my anger out. They ended up being quite homicidal.

LIFE

I was meant to take a life
by killing with a sharp knife.
No one will ever find the bodies of my victims.
There will not be a safe place for you to hide.
For when I go on my killing spree,
I will not spare a life.
Life is not worth living for—
that's what the crazy say.
But I'm not crazy; I just like
to live the murderous way.
Look out because you'll never be safe
from me and my gun,
and when I pull the trigger,
you won't be able to run.
I know this sounds demented;
I'll probably go to hell.
But I don't care one goddamn bit—
I just want to kill.

I wrote that on April 14, 1988. The people in my English class thought it was funny. The adults who saw it thought I was a psychopath. I really did have the desire to kill someone. The poems helped me pacify that urge. In class one day my friend Bridget was pissing me off, so I wrote her a sweet little poem.

KILLING BRIDGET

You push me just a little too far,
a little over the edge.
Well now you're going to pay the price—
I'll push you off a ledge.

I think you should be killed
by stabbing you in the face.
When they're looking for the killer,
there won't be any trace.

Maybe I should shoot you
to get it over fast.
No I think I'll let you suffer—
I want the pain to last.

Everyone got a kick out of that poem, because anyone's name can be put in instead of Bridget. Not too long after that, the school year ended, and I had yet another summer to spend with my two best friends, drugs and alcohol.

CHAPTER FOUR
▼

Chuck or Zack came over to my house almost every day during the summer before my sophomore year. When Chuck came he would call ahead for my "order." Usually I'd ask for a six-pack of 16-ounce beers, a fifth of Jack Daniel's, and a fifth of vodka. That would keep us happy from the morning until about five. I'd have pot to smoke with him, and sometimes he'd bring weed himself. If I had a full pack of cigarettes, too, I could be really happy. I always needed the cocaine, but I was hiding it from Chuck because ironically, he didn't approve of me doing it.

Tricia would sit in the backyard and watch us. I used to laugh about what the neighbors must have thought. The best days were when I could get drunk, stoned, and high. I thought I had the best life. I set fires in my backyard one day and put them out with the hose. I said I was playing fireman. There was one time when my grandfather came over to drop off a camera he had borrowed, and Chuck's motorcycle was in the driveway. I was drunk when he came, so I couldn't let him in. There were beer cans all over the house, and it smelled like pot. I just took the camera and said good-bye to him. After he left I took pictures of Chuck and Tricia. I still have those pictures. That night my grandfather called my mother to ask if she knew about the strange man in my house. She asked Tricia if I'd been drinking, and Tricia denied it.

The more unmanageable my life became the more I tried to escape from reality. One day after drinking at my house, Chuck and I went to Tricia's house with a couple of bottles. The three of us sat in her room. An hour later I got up and stumbled into the other room, where her brother and his friend were. I had a bottle of Jack Daniel's in my hand. His friend was disgusted and she told him she was leaving because her religion said drinking was sinful. She refused to be in the same house with people who were drinking. She told her mother, who called Tricia's father at work that afternoon. He came home and told me he was sick of my terrible influence on his children. I started to feel sick, so I poured my bottle into the sink and said I would never drink again. He told me not to come back unless I was completely sober. Later that day I was wishing that I hadn't dumped that bottle out.

Then I decided to try LSD again. I took three hits throughout one day and night. I thought it would be different because I wasn't taking them all at once. I also tried to put myself in a good state of mind. But my friends tried to get me violent, and the more obnoxious I got, the angrier I became. I was yelling and swearing. I wanted to pick a fight with someone so I could kick their ass. Finally I had a butcher knife at my friend's throat. Her boyfriend grabbed my arm and called me a crazy drug addict and told me I needed some serious psychiatric help. Then they left and I was alone. During the rest of the trip I sat in my room with the shades down and the door locked. I was paranoid. Every five minutes I thought someone was at the door, but no one was ever around. I wanted to cry, but I couldn't. I tried to sleep, but every time I closed my eyes, my eyelids would shake, and finally I just lay in my bed with my eyes open until the paranoia passed. It was a terrible trip. One of my friends stopped by later that night, and she was shocked to see what had happened to me. I lit up a joint as she left. She told me she hoped I would get some help. That was the last time I used LSD because I finally realized that I was placing myself in danger every time I took the drug. I'd stick to coke. Cocaine, alcohol, and marijuana weren't causing me any problems. Or so I thought.

When sophomore year began, I was only using cocaine one to three times per week. I wanted to start a drug program at Lauralton. I had this need to share my knowledge of drugs with other people. I wanted help to be available to anyone who wanted it. I wasn't sure what had to be done, but I was willing to do whatever was necessary. So my friends and I started a group called Students Against Drugs. I was the founding president.

At the same time, I was founding the Young Republicans Club as president. My first priority at the time was the Young Republicans, because the 1988 election was coming up soon. George Bush is a longtime idol of mine, and I'd known he would be the next president since eighth grade. I was a part of the Connecticut Republicans at age 15. I'd read Bush's book *Looking Forward* seven times. I was going to a Washington Workshops Congressional Seminar in January. I spent hours working at Republican headquarters, campaigning for George Bush and the local candidates. I went to a lecture given in Milford by William F. Buckley, Jr. I canvased for George Bush on a rainy day while my mother drove me from street to street.

November 7, 1988, was the night I had long awaited, the presidential election. I took the day off from school and reported to Republican headquarters in Milford. I was sent to a local polling place (a grammar school) to campaign. It was really cool. We had a friendly rivalry with the people representing the Democratic party. I took the bus home to West Haven around 4:00 P.M. I had a Sea Explorers meeting that night, and I brought Tricia because she wanted to join.

I was anxious that night. I'd joked with my parents, telling them that I was going to move to Canada if Michael Dukakis won the election. After the meeting, Tricia and I were supposed to go straight to the victory party at a Milford restaurant. Instead we went for a ride with Al. When we got to the party, I found out that I was late and my mother had been there looking for us. She was really pissed when Tricia and I finally caught up with her. We got into a huge fight in the car. She kept screaming at me, and she said, "The people in the Republican Committee think you're so great; they should see what you're really like." Then she said I wasn't worth the expense of going to the seminar in Washington. I flipped out. Tricia couldn't believe we were getting so pissed at each other. As soon as we got home I locked myself in my room and drank while I waited for the election results to be announced on TV. I threw a tape at my window and broke it. I didn't calm down until I found out that Bush had won.

After the election I had more time to devote to Students Against Drugs (SAD). That was when I first realized that there was something abnormal about my own drug and alcohol use. I didn't know what to do, though, so I just kept using. I was still smoking pot daily because I was substituting pot for cocaine in an attempt to control my cravings. About 50 kids joined SAD, but the school offered little support.

Chuck and I were arguing often because of my concern over his cocaine use. He was out of control, and wanted to date Tricia. He was 19; she and I were 15. There was a big difference between them in terms of maturity. She would have done anything to make him happy. She had tried cocaine, but I was afraid she would get heavily involved if she was in a relationship with him. I convinced her not to go out with him. He called me, crying over her decision. He didn't know I had a big part in her refusal. She came over to my house. He became very depressed and withdrawn.

One night Chuck came over to Tricia's house very drunk while we were there. I was sober at the time. He had his usual bottle of Jack Daniel's under his coat. But for some reason that disgusted me. When he asked me if I wanted a drink, I refused. I told him he was ruining his life, and that it wasn't going to get any better until he stopped using. We talked for a while, and by the time he was ready to leave, we were on good terms. The next night, he dropped a ring in Tricia's mailbox with a note that said he loved her. He told us to call him in a couple of days to make plans for his upcoming birthday.

For a couple of days I didn't know what had happened to him. Finally I called his house to see where he was. His brother answered the phone, and we talked for a while. Then I asked to talk to Chuck. He said, "He's dead." I thought that he was screwing around, so I said, "Come on, let me talk to him." He started screaming at me, calling me a heartless bitch. Then he was crying, saying he would never joke about anything this serious. I apologized and told him I'd call right back. As soon as I hung up, Tricia called. Through her tears, she told me about Chuck. Her parents had read his obituary in the paper. I tore through the paper looking for it. Before I could find it, I dialed the number of a bar down the street where he always hung out. The man who answered said, "Sorry, kid, we buried him this morning." Then I found the obituary and I was in shock. I found another article about him in the paper. I started crying. My parents and their friend Kevin walked into the room. I told them what had happened, and my mother said, "Don't worry, more of your friends are going to die before you do."

What happened was that Chuck had stolen thousands of dollars one day from his brother, Ray. He bought all the cocaine he could get, as well as liquor. He rented a motel room and prepared to freebase himself to death. He had a massive heart attack and fell down face first. He broke his nose and ended up leaning against a heater. Fourteen hours later, the maid found him dead, his right side severely burned. It was entirely premeditated. That night his friend Bill had driven him to the motel, and Chuck had said, "You'll be reading about me in the papers tomorrow." Bill hadn't taken him seriously. Chuck's brother almost beat Bill to death when he found out Chuck had told him what he was planning to do.

The week after Chuck died, I smoked crack for my first and only time. It was a Tuesday, right before a Sea Explorers meeting. Zack and I took the train up to New Haven and smoked in a parking lot.

I liked the crack high and everything about it: the crackling noise it makes when you smoke it, the smell. The smell isn't pleasant, but there's something I liked about it. I think I liked the wrong behind it. I knew that smoking crack was so "bad." It frightened me, though, the way my heart felt like it was going to explode. I was afraid to do it again.

Zack didn't go with me to the meeting, and when I arrived I went up to the pay phone to call him. I wanted him to meet me and get high after the meeting. I was carrying pictures of Chuck and his obituary. When the meeting was about to start, I showed Mrs. Holm the pictures. She asked how he'd died. I told her it was a cocaine overdose. She said, "Oh, well, then he deserved it."

I almost lost it right there. I said, "Fuck you. No one deserves to die, whether they did drugs or not. He had a problem." I felt like saying, I do the same drug, do I deserve to die? I'm surprised that I was able to control myself so well.

In early December Lauralton had its annual Mission Day, where the school puts on a sort of fair to raise money to send to missions. Instead of getting high, like I had the previous year, I led SAD in setting up a booth for publicity and raising money. It went well. Jill was the vice president, and since her mother owns a drugstore, she donated a box of pens that had "Just Say No" printed on them. We had one of the only game booths, and a local candy store had donated bags of candy as prizes. Many of our friends were drinking that day, but I restrained myself. I really didn't want to be a hypocrite. I was feeling accepted by my class, and if they knew I was using, Students Against Drugs would be a big joke. I didn't want it to be a joke. I was completely serious about the project.

At first I thought SAD would be a good cover, and that the school would never catch on to what I was doing. But it had become much more than that. It became my cause. I didn't want other kids my age to become drug addicts, even though at the time I couldn't accept that I was. I wanted to help people make healthier choices than I had made. If Sarah had been at Lauralton, I probably never would have started the club, but her mother had made her transfer to another school after freshman year.

Over Thanksgiving my aunt and cousin, Bonni and Jennifer, had moved in. Being an only child, I wasn't used to having other people living in the house. On December 10th the five of us moved to Milford. My mind was constantly focused on Chuck, death, and drugs. On December 13th I asked my father and Bonni to sign my organ-donor card as witnesses. When they all went out for dinner, I said I wanted to stay home. I prepared myself to die. I had been sharpening my favorite knife when my mother came in to ask if I wanted to go. I had purchased the knife on an eighth grade field trip to Boston. It was a black-handled butterfly knife. I sharpened it while listening to "The End," my favorite Doors song. I wrote a suicide note that was more like a will. It named people that my possessions should go to when I was dead. The note also said that I was sorry that things had turned out this way. When I felt the knife was sharp enough, I pulled a bottle of vodka out of my closet and started drinking it straight. I knew that my family wouldn't be home for a while. The phone began ringing as I walked downstairs, but I didn't answer it. I remembered that my friend Kelley was supposed to be calling; it was a Tuesday night and the Sea Explorers meeting had been canceled because of snow. I didn't want to give her the chance to talk me out of killing myself.

    I went down to the kitchen and laid out lines of cocaine on the counter. Before I did them, I filled two pots, one with ice-cold water and one with warm water. The plan was to numb my wrists with the ice water, make a deep vertical cut into the arteries on each wrist, then soak them in the warm water to make the blood flow faster. I snorted the lines and then stuck my arm into the ice water. I lit a cigarette and waited for my arm to numb. When it did, I took it out and dried it with a towel. Then I dug the knife deep into my arm. I put my arm into the warm water and sat on my kitchen floor with the phone. I called Kelley and she asked if there was something wrong.

    At first I tried to pretend like there wasn't, but then I started crying and I admitted to her that I wanted to kill myself. I didn't mention that I was in the process of doing it. I didn't want her to call an ambulance or anything. She made me promise not to do anything until she could get to my house. My cut had stopped bleeding long before she arrived.

    There was a big snowstorm that night, but her father

brought her to my house. She and I went for a walk in the snow around my neighborhood, and we decided that I should call Mr. and Mrs. Holm, our Sea Explorers leaders, for help. It sounded like a good idea at the time. I don't know what I expected them to be able to do for me. For quite a while after that I wore a long-sleeved shirt. In a way I was pissed because I had been convinced that I was going to die that night. I had thought that it was going to be over.

Three days later I went to the Holms' house to ask for their help. I'd just started a new job at a toy store for the Christmas season. Kelley had arranged a time with them around my work hours. Kelley and I were extremely nervous about going inside. The Holms had no idea what it was about. In fact, they hadn't even known they were meeting with me. I could tell they were really surprised about what I told them. They were more than willing to hear us out. We talked about my death wish for a little over an hour. I left out as much about drugs as I could. I think the only thing I admitted to was smoking pot on my first camping trip. The whole time we were there I was begging them not to call my parents. I honestly believed that my problems were minor and that I'd be able to straighten them out on my own. I promised to call them if the urge to kill myself ever came over me again.

The next day I had to go to work. I was still very depressed. I kept watching the clock, waiting for my break so that I could get high in the bathroom. I remember going out with my friends that night, but I drank heavily and had a blackout. The next day they told me I'd been an asshole.

The next Friday night, Kelley and I went over to the Holms' house again, and we baked cookies. I thought it was really cool. I had a lot of faith in them. They suggested to me that I go with them to see a pastor at their church. They thought he might be able to refer me to someone who could help me. The night we decided to go, I lied to my parents and said that I was going out with a friend from school. I felt really uncomfortable going. The idea of looking to a church for guidance bothered me. The pastor and I sat and talked about what was going on with me. I told him how I thought my life was worthless and how I wanted to die. We talked about my parents and about why I wasn't telling them anything. I didn't think my parents would understand at all. Toward the end of our meeting I started asking questions like was he a Democrat or a Republican. I was completely closed-minded about the opinions of any Democrat. He said that he was a Democrat. That was all I needed to hear to justify having an attitude. He did encourage the idea of my going to the cemetery to see Chuck's grave, though. That was something I wanted to do very badly. I felt like I had never gotten a chance to say goodbye to Chuck. I couldn't get rid of that feeling. Mr. Holm said they would take me.

The day before we went to the cemetery I received an invitation to the presidential inauguration from the 1989 Presidential Inaugural Committee. It made me feel good, but not good enough. I thought I would feel some great flood of emotion at the cemetery. I wanted to cry, but when I got there, nothing happened. I was numb. I had had this idea of bringing a bottle of Jack Daniel's to pour over the grave. I thought it would be what Chuck wanted. Mr. and Mrs. Holm didn't go for that idea. It was good for me to finally see where he was put to rest.

When I got home my mother wanted to know why they'd taken me there. It was hard to explain. I ended up telling her that the Holms just wanted to help since no one else was. That pissed my mother off. My parents had always hated it when I went outside the family with my problems. It reminded them of all the crap we'd gone through when I was in eighth grade. The next morning on the way to school, I told her I wanted to go to counseling. She reluctantly said okay, but never did anything about it.

On New Year's Eve I slept over at my friend Becky's house. I knew that Zack was going to come by and bring me some cocaine. Becky's parents weren't due home until early morning. I smoked pot, did lines, and drank as much as I could without getting sick. Shortly after midnight we went for a walk with our old friend Laura. I felt like I was crazy, as I did every time I mixed drugs like that. I was flipping out, giving Laura evil looks and telling her I wanted to kill someone. I scared her pretty badly. Becky was used to it from past experiences and knew enough to just humor me and leave me alone. That's the last time I remember seeing Laura.

During the first week of January 1989 I had yet another blackout. It was the night of a Sea Explorers boat work party. I drank a large quantity of Jack Daniel's before I went. It was sick the way I hid my drinking from everyone. I brushed my teeth about five times and chewed gum before I went. I didn't want anyone to smell the alcohol on my breath. I don't think anyone could've been sure I'd been drinking that night. All I remember after I got there was Mrs. Holm giving me a piece of paper with the number of the Milford Mental Health Clinic on it and telling me to make an appointment and they'd take me. The next day I spoke to the Holms and she said I'd been really obnoxious and aggressive, and that I was scaring them. Supposedly I had had money on me and had started walking to the train station and saying that I was leaving. I had told her that I'd made airline reservations for California and that I was going to live with my friend Sandy in San Diego. I couldn't recall any of this happening.

We had a snowstorm the next day and school was canceled. My cousin Jenn was home with me. Mrs. Holm and I made an appointment with the clinic. My mother called from work and I told her that I was going out to lunch with my friend and her mother. I was very nervous about going; I thought it was a terrible thing to have to go to a mental health clinic. I had to get high, I thought, because I didn't know how to handle such a situation. When we got there my heart was racing so fast that I thought I was going to have a heart attack. Mr. and Mrs. Holm went up with me to see a counselor. It was a woman. I never really liked talking to women about my problems. I felt much more comfortable talking to men. This lady was making me sick, talking to me like I was a toddler or something. We discussed how I was suicidal, but I minimized my involvement with drugs and alcohol, mostly because I was afraid to let the Holms find out about it. Then the psychiatrist came in to evaluate me. He came right out with, "I don't take any chances, and you seem to be in danger of hurting yourself, so I think you should be admitted to a hospital."

Now, all that was on my mind was the fact that I was supposed to be going to Washington, D.C., for the inauguration. There was no way in hell that I wasn't going. I made that real clear. Then they started in with, "Isn't your life more important than that?"

I said, "No, George Bush is more important."

There was also the point that it was my mother's birthday weekend. In the end, my decision was that I wouldn't go into the hospital no matter what, and at that moment they couldn't make me because I was only 15 years old and I was there without my parents' consent. It was decided that I would spend the weekend with the Holms because it was unknown how my parents would react to what was going on with me. On Monday my parents and I were supposed to come in for a meeting with the lady I didn't like.

On a normal day, my parents wouldn't have been home when I got to my house to get my clothes, but that day they happened to be there. Mr. and Mrs. Holm waited in the driveway for me while I went in. My mother was seriously pissed. Her anger was very visible by the redness in her face, and I think she would have blown up if she'd been any angrier. My mother went outside and told the Holms to leave, that they weren't taking me anywhere. She called both sets of grandparents. The ones that live in Milford came right over to get me. I couldn't put into words what was bothering me, so I couldn't tell anyone much. In my room, my grandmother said something like, "What are you trying to do, ruin our family name?"

I remember saying, "I don't care about your family name. Is that all you can think about?"

My grandmother felt bad and said that wasn't what she meant. In the middle of everything, Tricia called me. Of course, she didn't know anything was going on. My mother wouldn't hang up the phone she was on because she thought I would tell Tricia something she didn't know. I just told her I'd call her from my grandparents' house. I left to spend the weekend at their house, and it wasn't a pleasant situation. As I was walking out of my house my mother said, "Don't let the door hit you in the ass on the way out!"

When I got to my grandparents' house, it was like 20 questions at the dining room table. "Why would you want to kill yourself?" "Are you on drugs?" "Are your parents on drugs?" I spent the evening crying in my uncle's room. I was on the phone most of the night with Kelley and Mrs. Holm. I actually asked if I could go over to the Holms' house. Mr. Holm was willing to pick me up. I had a terrible headache and was craving cocaine. I hadn't taken any drugs with me. During the night I considered sneaking out and leaving, but I didn't. Since I wasn't high, I had some judgment. All I wanted to do was get high. At that moment, it wasn't suicide I was worried about. I needed drugs.

At my mother's birthday party the next day, things got a little better between us. It was at my house, so I brought all my stuff back from my grandparents' house and stayed home. Getting high was such a huge relief. The lady from Milford Mental Health had been calling all weekend to check on me. My parents didn't like it at all. When I was at my grandparents' house I heard my grandmother telling my mother that she wouldn't let me talk to the lady if she called back. I resented being treated like that. Things like that make me extremely angry. I can't deal with people trying to control me.

When Monday came I had the choice of going back to Milford Mental Health or not. I chose not to go. I didn't want to upset my parents more than they already were, so I called the clinic from school Monday and canceled my appointment. I never saw the counselor again. A couple of weeks later the clinic sent a letter to my parents warning them that I was at high risk for suicide and that they should take that seriously. Meanwhile, Bush's inaugural ball was coming up. Come hell or high water, I was going to Washington, D.C.

Up until I got on the plane, my parents kept telling me that I didn't have to go if I didn't think I could handle it. But I was all set. I'd taken my midterms at school a week earlier because I would have missed them during my trip. The only thing I was really nervous about was going away without drugs. I was too afraid of bringing them on the plane. I knew that, with a roommate, there was no way I could smoke pot in my hotel room. I doubted that she'd be a pot head. I didn't even want to risk bringing cocaine. After all the money that was invested in the trip, and the ticket to the ball, I couldn't back out.

I was glad to be taking a trip by myself. I needed to be

alone to sort things out. I flew down to Washington and got to where I was staying with no problem. It was a nice hotel on the campus of Georgetown University. I had to wait quite a while for my room assignment and registration, so I bought a pack of cigarettes and tried to take my mind off cocaine. I met my roommate. She was really cool. But one of the first things she said was that she hated people who do drugs. So I couldn't really relate or tell her how much I needed to get high.

After hanging around in our room for a little while, we took a walk. All I could think about was going home and getting some coke. I bought a roll of quarters and called Mrs. Holm from the pay phone. I told her I wanted to go home, and she thought I was crazy. There was no way I could say why. Was I supposed to tell her I was craving cocaine? I decided I wanted to come home the next day. I skipped the orientation that night and called my parents. They said I should wait a while and then decide if I really wanted to come back. I thought about it for a few hours, then I decided I needed to get home. It was hard to explain to everyone, so I said my grandmother had died. My parents were really confused. I couldn't find any way to explain why I wanted to leave.

From Washington National Airport I called my friend Wade, who had moved to Michigan the year before. He was disappointed, but he was one of the most understanding friends I had. I always felt comfortable talking to him because I knew he wasn't judging me. When I got home, everyone thought I was crazy. But I was getting high again, so I didn't care. I still regret not going to the inauguration, though.

My mother finally decided that I should see some kind of therapist. My aunt Jane, a psychologist, recommended one and my mother made me an appointment. I was glad to be going. For some reason I thought she would give me a clean bill of mental health and let me know I was fine. I was so sick of all the people around me thinking I was some kind of lunatic. As soon as I got there and sat down, she asked me why I thought I was there. I said, "I want to die."

That did it. I think a line like that tends to make people nervous. I mentioned that I thought I might have a drug problem, but she didn't address that. She wanted to stick to the depression. She had a theory that it was a chemical imbalance. I thought that might be true. When I left, I was under the impression that our session had gone well and that she wanted to help me. But the next night she called my mother and told her that I was too much for her to take on as a family therapist. She suggested that I go to the hospital for a psychiatric evaluation as soon as possible.

At school the next morning I was talking to Jill before homeroom. I told her I still wanted to kill myself, and I had a plan. I was going to paint a fingernail each day, and on the tenth day, I would kill myself. That morning the first one was painted. Father Doherty, a priest, overheard us, and asked me a few questions. He was trying to see how serious I was. I told him I was very serious, and that my time was up. I also let him know that I was planning to go for a psychiatric evaluation that day after school.

About ten minutes later I was in geometry. My guidance counselor pulled my teacher out of class to talk to her. I got nervous right away, and Jill was telling me, "She's here to see you." My friend Brooke seconded that thought. Everyone knew about my life, but they were all really supportive. Of course I did get pulled out of class, and as we were walking down the hall to her office, my counselor didn't say one word to me. She was pretty rude, like I was really ruining her day. She had a frown on her face and walked briskly. She directed me into the nurse's office and locked the door behind her. I said, "I'd unlock that door if I were you." She unlocked the door, and then she and the nurse started questioning me.

"Is it true that you're planning to commit suicide?" they asked.

"Who told you that? " I asked. "Father Doherty?"

"It doesn't matter how we found out," she replied. "Is it true?"

"It's none of your damned business what I do in my spare time," I said. "Don't worry, I won't make a mess here."

"Well, we've been told that you were supposed to go for an evaluation today," my counselor said. "We're going to have to call your parents and have them pick you up."

"I'll go after school," I told her.

"I'm afraid that's not possible," the nurse said.

"My aunt is home. Call her," I demanded.

"Your aunt isn't on the emergency card," the nurse claimed.

"Well, I'm putting her on it," I said, raising my voice. "Call her."

"We'll try your parents," she answered.

They called the office my parents work out of and had my mother paged. There was a wait, of course, until she could call back. There was no way I was going to let them call my grandmother and put her through that. I could feel my blood pressure rising. I asked to use a phone, and I went into my counselor's office. I really needed to talk to somebody and tell them what was happening. I dialed Mrs. Holm's work number. She wasn't surprised when I told her. Then I noticed my guidance counselor was still standing there, watching me. I started screaming, "Can I have some privacy, please?"

She said calmly, "Chris, I don't think you should be left alone right now."

After I hung up, I was pacing out in the hall, waiting for my mother to arrive. Then I was taken to get my books, which

Jill had brought to our second class, Health. It was my first Health class with the new teacher. What a great first impression she had of me, getting sent home for suicide risk. I walked right in, muttering under my breath about my guidance counselor being a bitch. Then I got all sarcastic and loud and explained to my class why I was being sent home. My guidance counselor was standing there getting really pissed. She said, "Let's go, Chris."

I said, "I'll go when I'm good and ready."

Mrs. Black, the teacher, seemed cool about it. She said, "What's your name?"

A girl said, "That's Chris Campbell. You'll know her soon enough."

When we got back upstairs, my mother was there, and she started telling my guidance counselor off, too. She said something like, "I'm sure it was important for her to go home now. She surely would have killed herself during the school day."

On the way to the hospital I prepared myself for the possibility of getting admitted to the psychiatric unit. When they interviewed me, I wanted to minimize my problems with both depression and drugs. We waited a long time to see someone from ACUTE, the Adolescent Crisis Unit for Treatment and Evaluation. A lady named Pam finally came and took my mother and me into a small office in the emergency room. We called my father to tell him to come. He knew something was going on because he'd been paged by my guidance counselor. We started answering questions before he arrived. I tried to make it sound like I was depressed but not suicidal. I kept repeating that I didn't want to kill myself. I knew how to answer questions like, "Do you have a plan for how you want to die?" When my father got there, the counselor asked him a few things. Then my parents left the room. I had to take a diagnostic test to determine my state of mind. I counted back from 100 by threes, told who the current president was, what hospital I was at, what city we were in. She told me an address, then changed the subject and a few minutes later asked me what the address was.

After the test I had to describe my chemical history, but I was far from honest. I admitted to smoking pot and drinking, but that was it. I told her I'd done LSD, but I asked her not to tell my parents because I knew she had to brief them on what I said. When she was finished asking me questions, I left and my parents came back in. I had to get a medical exam before I was through in the emergency room. The nurse who gave me my physical knew I was there for a psychiatric evaluation, so she asked me questions about what was wrong with me, too. I minimized with her, too.

Finally, after six hours at the hospital, Pam decided that I wasn't a danger to myself, that I had suicidal tendencies, but wasn't suicidal. She diagnosed me as having depersonalization disorder, told my parents I might have a drug problem, and referred me to a psychiatrist.

The spring semester was a difficult time for me in a few ways. I was frustrated with the school because they didn't seem to be at all interested in installing some kind of drug program. I was pushing to get Students Against Drugs off the ground. It had become more than a club. It was my mission. I wanted to save all my fellow students from drug problems. I tried very hard to get in touch with Dave Ullman, Milford's substance abuse coordinator at the time. I constantly asked the school administrators what they were doing to help our cause. I never let up on them to let me get more involved with anything that would give the group direction.

When I look back I can't believe I was still getting high

and at the same time wanting to help people. One day after school, Jill and the secretary, Nancy, and I went to talk to the superintendent of schools to ask about letting us speak to middle-school kids about substance abuse. I told him about our club and what our goals were. I said that we wanted to talk to seventh- or eighth-grade kids about drugs. I didn't think we were getting anywhere. It was immensely frustrating. It seemed like we were kids and nobody cared about what we thought because we couldn't vote.

Those who knew I was using called me a hypocrite, but I didn't think that was true. I really wanted to keep other people from using drugs. I didn't realize it at the time, but I couldn't stop using. But for the first time, I tried to stop. That was when my physical problems started.

During late February Zack stopped using and dealing. I decided that I should try quitting, too. I cut down until I was only doing cocaine about twice a month. I managed to do that for two months. It was terrible for me. I felt like I was living hell on earth. I started to have partial seizures. I didn't know that I was having seizures at first, but I knew there was something wrong with me. Every day without fail I had terrible headaches, and they never went away. I'd wake up and go to sleep with a headache. Then one of my teachers mentioned to me that sometimes I was losing attention in her class for no reason. She would say something to me, and I wouldn't respond. For about 20 seconds or so, someone would be saying, "Chris, Chris," and I wouldn't answer. As soon as I regained consciousness, so to speak, I'd have an almost unbearable headache. It was scary. And it seemed to be getting worse. I mentioned it to the psychiatrist I'd started seeing in February.

I never mentioned to my psychiatrist that I was doing cocaine. I'd told him that I'd experimented with the drug, but that was it. I saw him twice a week from February to late April. I didn't like him much at all. I'd sit in front of him, and he wouldn't speak unless I spoke first. I never knew what to talk about, so a lot of time was spent just staring at each other. My parents didn't like him, either. When he theorized that I was having partial, or petit mal, epileptic seizures, my parents were surprised. It was just another surprise for them. The psychiatrist recommended a neurologist.

In March I had a CAT scan, but it revealed nothing. In April I had a portable electroencephalograph, EEG, that I wore for 24 hours. I was extremely nervous about all these tests because I thought for sure that I was going to be diagnosed as having epilepsy. My psychiatrist told me it was likely that I wouldn't be getting my license to drive in May as I'd planned. I said that I would because the state wouldn't know that I had seizures. Then he told me it was his duty as a physician to inform them if I had epilepsy.

It still never occurred to me that any of my problems were drug related. I didn't really know that cocaine could cause seizures. I never mentioned any drug use to my neurologist. He said there was nothing he could do for these seizure-like episodes, but that my headaches were probably caused by stress. He said that if the seizures got any worse, I'd have to be admitted to the local VA hospital for a special test that might last up to a week. I never had to do that though, because I started using cocaine daily again, and the seizures stopped. Right before I did though, I had a seizure in biology lab at school, and Jill was my lab partner. It really freaked us out. It was one of the worst I'd had. But suddenly the seizures just stopped, and no one had a clue why.

My 16th birthday was March 30, 1989. I asked for golf clubs because I knew that I wasn't going to get a car. Golf, tennis, and hockey have always been my favorite sports. My birthday was on a Thursday, and my parents had my friends from Sea Explorers come over for a surprise birthday party. It was nice. I got my golf clubs, which made me happy. I also got my license permit that day, even though the seizure thing hadn't been resolved yet. I hadn't taken Driver's Ed, and I wanted to get my license as soon as possible.

That Saturday I got a present from my friend Joe that I thought was the best thing I could've received at the time. We went for a ride and stopped at the beach. He told me to go for a walk and come back. I was paranoid because I thought he was going to leave me there or something. I went for a little walk and smoked a cigarette. When I got back, he had the back of his Blazer open. Inside there was a mirror about two feet long. It had "Happy Birthday, Chris" spelled out in cocaine. I couldn't believe it. We sat there for a while, snorting it and smoking butts. I offered him money, but he said, "It's your birthday. Enjoy it." He was dealing, so I wasn't worried about him needing the money. I was high the whole weekend, including at my family birthday party. I thought it was really cool to spend my 16th birthday wired on cocaine.

At school Mrs. Black, the Health and Gym teacher, started asking me questions. All the time during my French class I used to sit in her office and she'd ask me about what it was like to be high on different drugs. Then one day she told me that people who do coke have no consciences, that they never feel guilty about the things they do while they're high. That bothered me, because around that time I had begun stealing quite a bit to support my cocaine habit. I had to, because Zack was no longer there to give it to me. I was able to steal money from Becky's parents, because they kept a box of money from which I could snag a few 20s at a time. They never noticed. I sold my things in order to get money, and whenever there was an opportunity to get cash I never passed it up. If it wasn't nailed down, I'd take it. So when Mrs. Black said that, it really pissed me off. I felt really guilty about the things I did. I told her that I didn't do cocaine anymore, but that I'd done a lot of it in the past. In class, she'd pretend she knew all about coke, and sometimes she'd pick on me to talk about it. I didn't want my classmates to know about my drug use. I didn't trust anyone enough to tell them what I was doing. As it was I was still concerned that they were going to put me in the hospital over the suicide issue.

Two great things happened to me during the first week of May. I decided to run for junior class treasurer, but I didn't take it seriously. I didn't campaign at all. The two girls I ran against put up posters all over the school. I just told my friends that I had my name on the ballot. By the election everyone knew I was running. I got nervous because I heard two seniors in the hall talking about how class elections were nothing but a popularity contest. The day of the election we had to give speeches, and I had nothing prepared. The class moderator, Sister Mary, was shocked when I told her I was planning to give a speech off the top of my head. I knew it would be much more sincere if I just got up there and said what I felt.

A couple of days before the election, the school business manager accused me of stealing $14,000 of school funds. She claimed I smuggled them into the SAD bank account. I didn't even know SAD had a bank account. The whole thing was ludicrous. I had to laugh, because it was such a good idea. It was a pretty serious accusation, and they ended up apologizing and clearing up the situation. But I felt like the school scapegoat.

The day I made my speech, Sister Mary decided that the treasurer candidates should go first, and why not start with Chris, the class clown? The assembly was in the chapel, and I just walked up to the altar and started. I told them that there was no reason for them to vote for me because I was probably the most irresponsible member of the sophomore class. But I would make class meetings fun, and they should vote for me because I was great. Well, they loved it, especially when I threw in the accusation of my stealing from the school. It was a real ego boost for me when everyone screamed for me after my speech. At the end of the day, when it was announced that I'd won, I couldn't believe it. I got this rush of self confidence that was the beginning of a great relationship with everyone in my class.

Later that week I got my driver's license. I'd been dying to drive. It was a little more than one month after my 16th birthday. My friends and I drove around in my father's truck for six hours that day. I was so excited. I felt so cool that I was driving a standard shift car right away, too. As soon as I got the courage to drive to the projects, it made it easier to buy drugs.

At the end of the year I felt an enormous burden of guilt about my involvement with SAD. Ninety-five percent of the members were under the assumption that I wasn't using drugs at all. They thought I had been a substance abuser at one time but had stopped and was now drug free. I tried very hard to keep my personal life a secret. Then my fellow members wanted me to impeach Jill and Nancy as officers. Rumors around school were that they smoked pot frequently. I laughed to myself about what everyone would say if they found out I was doing cocaine every day. Smoking pot was nothing to me. But I felt I had no choice but to say something because the club meant so much to me. I put it off for as long as I could. Then one day the three of us were in the locker room and I told Jill and Nancy how the members of the club felt. I tried to make it sound like I didn't share that opinion, because I didn't. They were still pissed at me, though, calling me a hypocrite. They both knew that I used, although they thought I was just smoking pot. I stopped telling anyone at school what I was doing.

CHAPTER FIVE
▼

Right before school ended, my Religion teacher told our class that when we returned in the fall, things would be different. We would be more mature. She said it was the summer before junior year that matured students. I was wondering if I'd be shooting heroin by the end of the summer.

I actually didn't want the year to end. I loved school. My duties as treasurer had already started. We were planning the prom for the next year. I was really happy about my decision to go to Lauralton Hall. I was working at a gas station, a longtime ambition of mine. I thought it was cool for a girl to be pumping gas. I got fired though, for taking too much time off. My boss sent my last check with a note stuck on it that said, "Good luck." During the summer I worked at an ice cream store right down the street from me. I really liked the job because it was very close to my house and in a good location for my friends to visit.

In July my neurologist put me on the prescription antidepressant Elavil for my headaches. At first I didn't like it because it made me very drowsy. But after a while my body got adjusted to it and it helped my headaches a lot. The doctor warned me about drinking while taking the pills, but I kept on using cocaine and marijuana as usual.

The weekend I started on Elavil, the Sea Explorers took a trip up to Camp Sequassen without the Holms. Al and I were stoned the whole time. We slept nine people in a lean-to meant for four. We had a great time. About a week after that trip, we took a Sea Explorers trip to Long Island for a week. The first thing I did when I got off the boat at the first port was go smoke a joint with Al. Then we took a two-mile walk into town to get a pizza because we had the munchies. All day on the sail I'd been dying to get high. I guess I was really obnoxious and morbid throughout the whole trip, especially when I wasn't getting high. One night we stayed in Sag Harbor. Just to get a buzz I bought a box of Vivarin and a six-pack of Jolt cola. I bought a fishing knife in Greenport and had it for about an hour before it got taken away from me for good.

The night after that I was sitting on the deck of the boat with Sara, Keren, and Al, talking about how I wanted to take my fishing knife and just stick it in my head or someone else's head. Mrs. Holm started yelling at me, telling me that she was going to call my parents and send me home because she couldn't deal with me anymore. That night I took three Elavils—the dose I was supposed to ease up to—and I practically passed out. I never got that knife back, although I don't blame them. I wouldn't give me a knife. I would get in these really strange suicidal, homicidal moods. I never thought about what I said or did before I did it. I was going crazy the whole trip because I didn't have any cocaine.

That summer Al and Mark came over to my house almost every day. Usually they rode their bikes over because none of us had cars. We'd get baked and drink, especially Al.

He loved vodka. There was always a bottle of vodka in my house. My cousin Jenn was home with us all the time, too. She thought we were all really strange.

Whenever I could, I'd use. Anything I could get my hands on. I didn't care if all I could do was suck the air out of a whipped cream can.

Right before school started in the beginning of September, I started seeing a neuropsychologist, Dr. Bob Novelly. Before I met him I had begun to get the idea that all psychologists were assholes. But he was a real cool guy, nothing like any of the other mental health professionals I'd seen. I really liked him. My parents liked him, too, so it was cool. When I went to him, my anger came out, maybe because he was the only person I could do that with. Sometimes I felt like I wasn't accomplishing anything, but that certainly was not the case. He was the first person to help me realize that suppressing my emotions was a real issue for me, that it led to my becoming a very angry, hostile person. Since I was forcing myself to avoid my feelings, I wasn't cognizant of the person I had become, angry and hurt. Because of what he told me about my anger, I started writing a journal. I wanted to get in touch with where my anger was coming from.

Since I never brought it up, we hardly ever discussed my drug and alcohol use. This was partly because I didn't see any problem with it. I did admit to using alcohol and smoking pot. I rarely talked about cocaine, though. I guess I tried to make it sound like I had done it before, but not for any length of time. I was more interested in my suicidal depression than my drug abuse. He tried to get me to talk about my parents and what they were like, but I never wanted to. I didn't want to say anything bad about my parents, and at that point I couldn't think of anything nice to say. I wasn't at all afraid to tell him what I was feeling. I trusted Bob, because I knew he wasn't going to send me to the hospital the first time I mentioned suicide. He didn't treat me like a two-year-old.

By September, I felt like a new person. Of course, I was still doing cocaine daily, along with other drugs. But 11th grade was great. I had two honors classes, and I loved being in them. I dropped French, which I hated, and took Spanish, which I enjoyed.

We had to keep a religion journal, which I didn't mind. I honestly enjoyed Religion class. Even though I didn't believe in God, I liked to learn about morality and values. We had a lot of good class discussions. We talked about Anne Frank, whom I really admire. I understood what my teacher meant about reading her when you doubt your happiness, because I did the same thing with George Bush. Whenever I doubted my success in something like my future, I looked over his book and it encouraged me to keep going. I thought about becoming a politician someday. I felt it was my "mission" to serve my country as a leader. I thought it was funny to have this good attitude suddenly.

I was having the best time ever at school. I had the best grade average I'd had since high school began. I loved all my classes. I was taking honors History and English. I felt like I had some power and status because I was a class officer, and president of my own club. I enjoyed speaking to the class during class meetings. In fact, I loved public speaking.

My drug use had not declined at all. I was doing cocaine as much as ever. I drank no less than before, and I smoked pot on every possible occasion. I missed the old days of my using though, because I was having great guilt over getting high now. I was still involved in drug prevention. But I felt that my use was justified because of all the responsibilities I had. I would go to work at the ice cream store, bring my homework, and actually do it. I hadn't done homework regularly since eighth grade. My teachers all liked me because I participated positively in class, a switch from the year before. In the very beginning of the school year, Mrs. Gates, the dean of students, had approached me and said that Dave Ullman wanted to meet me about the drug program to be implemented in the school.

I was excited because I had been waiting a long time for this. The whole drug curriculum meant a great deal to me. I didn't want kids to get involved in drugs like I had. I didn't feel like a hypocrite at all. It seemed like I was doing something worthwhile, even if I myself couldn't stop using. Things began looking up for my club when the Boy Scouts' district executive told me about a new group called Drug Free Milford. He told me the date of the first meeting. I went with Jill, Tricia, and Al. As soon as we walked into the meeting, we met Dave Ullman. I stood up during the meeting and introduced myself as a student at Lauralton Hall and the founding president of Students Against Drugs. I told the roomful of people how badly the school needed a drug-prevention curriculum, and how I was frustrated with the whole system. Dave and I talked after the meeting and we made plans to meet and discuss my ideas for SAD.

A few days later I had my first cocaine overdose. My heart was beating so fast that I thought it was going to explode. I couldn't breathe because it hurt too much, like I was going to have a heart attack. Everything was white and I was really dizzy. I coughed up this white foam and blood. My friend called it a "whiteout." I honestly thought I was going to die. But when it was over I asked for more coke. I even told everyone that it felt cool, and they should try to OD.

I spoke to the Milford Women's Club in early October about the drug and alcohol problem among today's youth. I was really honored that they asked me to speak to their group.

I had never done anything quite like that before. I tried to make it sound like I didn't know what it was like to actually use but had heard what it was like. I didn't want to come off as a user myself. At school the administration was concerned that I would bad-mouth Lauralton and say that they didn't care about the problem, and essentially I did just that. The women wrote a letter and sent it to Lauralton saying that they liked what I had to say and that they supported me. Mrs. Gates and Mrs. Johnson, the principal, agreed with Mrs. Black to let Jill and me start working on a presentation to the freshman Health classes. We were to do it in mid-November. We would deal with alcohol, marijuana, cocaine, and hallucinogenics. What amazes me now is that I did all that research on these drugs and chemical dependency and never realized that I had a problem.

When Dave Ullman came to Lauralton to see the SAD officers about the drug curriculum in the school, Mrs. Gates made an announcement opening up our meeting to anyone who wished to attend. That really annoyed me because I didn't even want the administrators there, let alone kids in the school that weren't in our club. It started out okay, but then, as usual, I began going off on the administrators. We really didn't get anything accomplished. Mr. Ullman had me call him that night. He told me that I had to be patient, that things like drug programs didn't happen overnight, and I was getting too angry at the faculty. He was right. I didn't have any patience with them at all. I would just go off and start yelling as soon as things didn't go my way.

We had a mass in school right before Halloween. My friend Brooke and I refused to stand up during mass. It was our protest against Catholicism. I realize that it was a pretty childish thing to do and very disrespectful. I was supposed to be a role model as a class officer. I was setting a bad example for the freshmen. But when it was time to stand, we remained seated. We were in the last row, and since the faculty sat behind the students, one of the sisters saw us. She came up and started yelling at us. "How could you be so disrespectful?" she screamed. "I don't care if you're Catholic or not," I heard her saying to another teacher, "I don't know what is wrong with that girl, she has such an attitude." But I didn't care if I was being rude.

I started writing my journal right after Halloween because I had an incident occur that really illustrated to me how out of control my anger sometimes became. It was the first year that all of the classes, not just the seniors, could wear Halloween costumes. I wanted to wear something that I thought everyone would expect. So I was Jason from the Friday the 13th movies. I wore old clothes, boots, and a mask, and brought a gun with no trigger. I also had a plastic pitchfork. The gun got a lot of attention. It happened to be the last day of a visit from the people evaluating the school. After lunch I was walking upstairs with a couple of my friends. The gym teacher, Mrs. Black, called me back down to her. She wanted to see the gun. It was pretty obvious that I had it because I was wearing a holster. Mrs. Johnson was standing close by with the visitors. Mrs. Black took the gun and brought it over to them.

That really pissed me off because I didn't see anything wrong with having it. They told me it was inappropriate to bring a gun to school, trigger or no trigger. They said I could come and get it after school. I called Mrs. Johnson a bitch and started going off on both of them. I took the gun back, and Mrs. Johnson went to take it away, but I wouldn't let go. She kept saying over and over, "Give me the gun, Chris." I finally just gave it to her. My friends dragged me downstairs. When I got back to the cafeteria, there were already stories about what had happened. Some people said that I hit her, but I didn't.

When I went to get the gun after school, Mrs. Johnson wasn't too pleased with me. The administrators never forgot that incident. Just to make things a little more tense, I started bringing *Gun World* magazine to school.

It was mid-November when Jill and I were finally going to give our presentations to the freshman Health classes. That week, Mrs. Gates, the dean, and Mrs. Black, set up a meeting with us in Black's office, which was a pretty small room. I perceived their attitudes immediately as denying us the chance to talk to the younger kids. I think the size of the room made a difference in the tension between us. Mrs. Black sat behind her desk. I sat in a chair in front of her desk. Gates sat facing me against the wall. Jill stood by the door against the wall. As soon as our meeting started, Mrs. Gates told me it was probably a mistake to let us talk to impressionable students because I was "immature and irresponsible." At that point I could feel my blood pressure rising. Jill was giving me these looks that said, "Stop, don't get angry." I got up out of my chair with my fist raised and almost punched Gates. I paced around the room quickly, then sat back down. Gates went on to say, "See? You can't handle this." I jumped up again and punched the wall. Then I put my hands around Jill's neck and it must've looked like I was going to strangle her. I kept saying, "Jill, I'm going to kill her."

Mrs. Black tried to be tough, leaning forward at her desk, and said, "Chris, you don't understand."

That was all I could handle. I slammed my hands down on her desk and yelled, "No, *you* don't understand." I walked out into the hall, where Mrs. Black's class was waiting. I was yelling at them from out in the hall, "Immature and irresponsible? Do you think I'm immature and irresponsible?" It was scenes like this that made them wonder if I could handle situations where people confronted me. As soon as things looked like they weren't going my way, I'd go off.

On November 16 Jill and I made two presentations. Black and Gates had decided to take a chance and let us speak to two classes after we did a mock presentation for the two of them. Mrs. Black liked them and told Gates that they went well and that it hadn't been a mistake to let us do them. Mrs. Black liked the first one better than the second because, according to her, we were too casual in the second one.

Then Mrs. Gates gave Jill a detention for skipping Driver's Ed the day before.

The next day, Friday, I was walking around the school bitching about Mrs. Gates and calling her every name in the book. Then I went into the lunch room and told some of my friends that I wanted to slash Gates's tires. At the time I was kidding. I never had any intention of going through with it. But while Jill and I were out that night, the perfect opportunity arose for revenge. It was the night of the senior dance, and we knew that Gates would be there. Jill's sister, Missy, was a senior and was at the dance. I got my knife and we drove to Lauralton. We left a note on Missy's car that said we had "done it," which she would understand. We were too excited to keep the news to ourselves, and we thought that our secret would be safe with Missy. There was a cop walking around the grounds. As soon as he left the area of Gates's car, I pulled up to her car. Jill jumped out and slashed the tires. Then she got back in and we drove away. When she got in the car I said, "Did you do it? Did you do it?"

"Can't you hear it?" she yelled.

She'd done it, but I think we both had second thoughts when she got back into the car. Jill was sober, but I had snorted about a gram of cocaine while getting the knife at my house. Over the weekend we reassured ourselves that there was no way we could get caught for doing it. The night of the dance, however, Missy went to a party drunk, and while she was on the phone with Jill, she yelled, "Jill slashed Gates's tires!" to a roomful of Lauralton seniors. So they all knew we had done it. Jill and I asked Kate, our friend, to cover for us if we were questioned on Monday. We knew it would be very likely that the school would suspect us because of our history of troublemaking. Kate was supposed to say that her boyfriend did it because he didn't like Gates. It was a pretty weak alibi, but we had no alternatives.

In school on Monday during homeroom an assembly was called right away for the seniors. All the juniors were walking around the homerooms trying to figure out what was going on. Jill and I were practically having heart attacks because we knew exactly what was happening. The administration told the seniors that they would lose their privileges if they didn't tell who slashed the tires. We knew that none of Missy's friends would tell, but we couldn't be sure about the rest of the seniors. Mrs. Gates never would have suspected Jill and me, but to cover I went up to her and showed her my report card. I knew she would be happy that I got three A's. I also told her that I had heard people were accusing Jill and me and I wanted to make it clear that it wasn't true. She believed me. But toward the end of the school day, more and more people started to figure out that Jill and I were the ones. Mrs. Black told me that she suspected it was us, but she hoped we weren't capable of doing something so terrible. Jill had detention after school. Gates, Johnson, Black, and Walker, the dean of studies, called her down to the boardroom to have a meeting. They asked her if she was the one who did it. They asked her if she knew anything at all about it. Then Mrs. Johnson warned Jill that if she admitted it now, it would be a lot easier than if they found out some other way. It was like they were out for blood or something. They were trying to scare us into admitting it.

The next day was the last day of school before Thanksgiving vacation. That morning I was called down to see Mrs. Black. She asked me if we were the ones. I tried to look all insulted that they would even ask me. I pulled out *Hot Rod* magazine and started yelling at her that I love cars and would never slash the tires on a Saab. It wasn't the Saab, however—it was another one of her cars—but I thought it would look like I didn't know. She told me that Jill had been identified as the one who did it, and that meant I was probably involved somehow. I denied over and over that I had anything to do with it. I thought I was going to get away with it. I went down to the art room to talk to Jill, but the teacher didn't like me, so she kicked me out. I went to my class. Third period I had a big chemistry test. In the middle of it, Miss Walker came and pulled me out. I knew I was screwed right there. I tried to make small talk with her, but she wasn't in the mood. We walked through the administration building into a part of the school that was rarely used. That made me suspicious because she had said that Mrs. Gates wanted to talk to me, but we walked right past her office.

She led me into a small room, and a police officer stood up to greet me. We sat down, and he informed me that he knew I was one of the perpetrators of the crime. I wouldn't admit to it, and he ended up reading me my rights three times before he gave up. He was frustrated and told Walker he couldn't do anything unless we confessed. Miss Walker brought me into her office and left me alone to call my parents. After I left a message at their office I just sat there. I was very nervous, and I was wondering what Jill was doing. Miss Jones, the Religion teacher, came in and sat down with me. When she told me I was probably going to get kicked out of Lauralton, I started crying. She said that a statement to the police had been signed saying that Jill and I had slashed the tires. She said, "Chris, I can't believe you were involved in this."

Then Mrs. Johnson came in and said, "Jill told us you did it, Chris." Later I found out that they had walked in and said, "Chris told us you did it, Jill." They were playing us against each other.

Johnson asked me, "Are you seeing someone, Chris?" meaning a psychiatrist.

Then they finally got in touch with my mother. She left work to come to the school. While a senior assembly was called, I sat in a secluded section of the main office, and Jill sat in the public part. They wouldn't let us talk to each other. The seniors were told that the people who slashed the tires were sitting in the office, and the senior class got their privileges back. Mrs. Black came in and asked me if there was anything she could do. I said I wanted to talk to Jill. "Well, I don't think that's possible right now," she said and walked out.

After what seemed liked days my mother finally arrived. I sat down with her, Gates, and Johnson. They said I was suspended indefinitely, and I might be asked to withdraw. I didn't feel like it was really happening. Then Mrs. Johnson told me that what we did was a heinous crime, and it probably would not "benefit the Lauralton community for me to return there." When I got home I called Jill's house. Missy answered. She said she had told Johnson off because she was in the room with Jill and their mother when they had their meeting. Johnson had told her mother that she thinks that there is something very wrong with Jill to make her do something like slash tires and feel no remorse. They said she had no remorse because Jill wasn't really outwardly upset about the whole situation and I was. Then I talked to Jill. She was depressed. Neither of us could believe it was happening. The next morning both Mrs.

Black and Miss Jones called my house to see if I was all right. It really bothered me the way that they favored me over Jill because they expected something like that from her but not me. I was very sad. I loved Lauralton and I didn't want to switch schools. I cried every time I thought about it.

My parents were really cool about my situation at Lauralton. They knew that I was upset enough with the prospect of having to leave without them being pissed at me as well. They were very supportive about it. They gave me the leeway to just be alone; I didn't want to be around any other people. Jill's parents were not quite as accepting. I was so thankful that my mom and dad weren't bitching me out. I don't think I could've handled that.

After the holiday break, I got my first letter asking me to withdraw because of my "actions and repeated refusals to own up to my responsibility." That night I got high, of course, because that was the only way I knew how to handle such a situation. It felt so frustrating because there was nothing we could do but wait and see if they would reconsider. I kept getting high, over and over, until I passed out. The next day we tried to get them to reconsider. I wrote in my journal that if there was a God, Jill and I would get back into Lauralton. The only time I ever prayed was when I was trying to make something go my way. On November 29, 1989, I got my answer from Lauralton. The school sent this letter by certified mail so that we wouldn't have to wait. It gave me a week to withdraw or face expulsion.

I felt like I was going crazy. I got high immediately. I did about a gram of coke. I grabbed the biggest knife I could find, then ripped the knife into my arm, over the scar I had from the previous year. I didn't bother to numb it this time. I wanted it to hurt. Then I called Jill. We talked for a while. I told her what I had done, and then I said I wanted to stop the bleeding and

I'd call her back. I called Mrs. Holm and told her that I had gotten kicked out of school, then left a message for Dr. Novelly to call me. I went upstairs to call Jill. The bleeding had stopped. I put on a long-sleeved shirt because I didn't want to look at the gash I now had on my arm. The doorbell rang. I thought it was Al; I had forgotten he was in New York for the day. It was Mrs. Black. I don't know why, but I was really rude to her. Just the fact that she was associated with Lauralton made me sick. She asked if I wanted to go for a ride with her, but I said no. I didn't let her in or anything. I said I wanted to be alone. This is what I wrote that day:

> *I know that withdrawing from Lauralton isn't enough to die, but since I hate everything else about life I don't see why I just don't do it. I hope it happens soon. If I try to die I don't want to only make it half way.*
>
> *I ripped my arms apart again. It's not even that I don't want to go to another school, I just really loved Lauralton. I can't handle this. If it wasn't for drugs I don't know what I'd do. That's all I have, the ability to get high. I hate life, and I hate that school for doing this to me. I feel like a real-life Holden Caulfield.*

For the next week I tried to think of another private school I could go to, but nothing worked out. I agreed with my parents that I would go to the public school, Joseph A. Foran High School. I was nervous about it, because I hadn't been to a public school for a while. I was happy in a way because I thought there would be more drugs than there were at Lauralton.

My first day at Foran was December 4, 1989. I made a very important decision that day. I decided that I wanted to become a doctor again. In eighth grade I had pretty much forgotten about my ambition to pursue medicine. But suddenly I realized that it was what I wanted to do. I had always wanted to be a doctor. In grammar school I had the nickname Doc Chris because I was always reading books on medicine. It was drugs, mainly, that led me away from my original ambitions. I didn't care about the future. I only cared about getting high. When I started at Foran, suddenly my future became important to me. But not important enough for me to stop using. I didn't look forward to going to school anymore. It was a strange place. I didn't know anyone but Al and two other Sea Explorers, Keri and Kevin. They were seniors and I was a junior, so we didn't have any classes together, except Al and I had the same study hall.

My motivation for doing well at Foran was the hope that Lauralton would let me return for my senior year. It was Mrs. Gates who told me I might be able to go back.

In mid-December I told Mr. Holm that I had done cocaine in September and that was what led to the disagreement I had had with his wife. I tried to make it sound like an isolated incident. I'm not sure what made me bring it up. I think that in a way I wanted to tell them how much I was using. No matter what was going on around me, cocaine was my first love. Nothing else mattered if I had coke.

> *December 2, 1989:*
> *I had a good session with Dr. Novelly. He's a real nice guy. It always makes me feel better to go, so he must be doing something right. This week I'm supposed to pay attention to where my hurt and anger are coming from. I guess I can't really start solving the problem until I find the source. He said next year when I reapply at Lauralton he'll send a letter saying I've improved and all that shit. He tells me that I'm not*

crazy, I'm just angry and hurt.

I'm pleased to report that the marks on my arms are healing quite nicely. Maybe they won't leave too much of a scar. I suppose that would be nice so I don't look so suicidal.

December 20, 1989:
My grandfather has a brain tumor. Could this year be worse? I wish I could be more apathetic so I wouldn't feel so bad. Right now I take back everything I said about my parents and my grandparents. I think they do deserve better than me. They try so hard to make me happy. Someday I'll be able to fulfill a lot of things for everyone.

Right after Christmas I had the urge to volunteer somewhere, and I tried the local homeless shelter. They wouldn't take me because I was only 16. I also started thinking about working as a volunteer at a hospital, but I didn't want to be a candy striper. My opportunity came in January, when the Yale-New Haven Hospital Outreach Program came to my school. They basically talked about careers in health care, but there was a part on volunteering. I signed up to participate in the program. I ended up making an appointment for an interview later in the month. My goals at that point were to: 1. get back into Lauralton. 2. get accepted at Tulane University. 3. complete a premed program. 4. start medical school.

My relationship with my parents was good, but it had its ups and downs. I wanted things to get back to normal, and it wasn't going as smoothly as I'd wanted.

December 28, 1989:
I wish my mother would learn that I wasn't put on

this earth to read her mind. She should live her own life and realize that if my father forgets their anniversary, it isn't my problem. I have my own life. I would be happy if I was an unfeeling, apathetic person. No one understands me. I don't even understand me. I feel like someone else is living my life and I'm just watching. It's like I have no part in this—I'm just an observer.

I don't think my mother knows that I almost hate her for what she does to me. It's selfish the way she never paid any attention to me when I had a problem. How can she deny that there could ever be a problem with me? I don't seem that infallible, do I? Even when I came right out and said I wanted to die last year she ignored me.

January 25, 1990
Well I can't say I didn't learn anything today. I was right all along. I'm going to stop kidding myself and accept the fact that I am worthless and my life will never be anything but worthless. I can look at this as the day I gave up. From now on I don't care what happens. I don't plan on sticking around. It's no use for me to keep living a life of rejection and failure. I want to die, and there is nothing wrong with that. I'm not going to allow my mother to play head games with me any longer. I hate my parents and I'm not going to feel guilty when I kill myself. I won't feel anything. No one really cares so why should I? Why keep living a life that makes me so unhappy? As soon as it'll be successful I'll make my move. I hate my parents and I hate myself. She's right, I am unbalanced, and thanks to them I'll never be another way. So I guess I'll just

join the other failures who have committed suicide. I don't want someone to help me, I just want the world to leave me alone. If I can't be happy, then I won't let myself feel unhappy either. I never really asked for much. And I never got what I asked for either.

I started volunteering at Yale-New Haven Hospital in early February. Since I presented myself as a responsible leader type, I got a job on the Adolescent Unit as a student health care preceptor. This meant that I followed the nurses and doctors in order to learn about professional health care to prepare for a future as a doctor. At first, psychiatry and neurology were what interested me most, but that changed. Cancer patients interested me more. I sought to learn as much about oncology as I could. I often went in to talk to the oncology patients, and I read their charts at every opportunity. The nurses taught me as much as they could about chemotherapy and other cancer treatments, and about the disease in general. I worked on a project dealing with acute leukemia. It fascinated me to the point of not wanting to learn about anything else. I wanted to spend all of my free time at the hospital. I was reading about oncology constantly. I ignored my schoolwork and concentrated on hematology and oncology.

The hospital was a place where I found something in myself that I had always known existed. I wanted to help people. I felt a great need to be there, to be involved in the healing process. However, the hospital also provided me with something else that I needed desperately—clean syringes and needles. It is very difficult to obtain clean sets for shooting drugs intravenously. Until I began working at the hospital, I shared a lot of dirty needles with people that I barely knew. Cleaning a set with bleach was not on my mind when I was about to get high. The thrill of cocaine in my bloodstream outweighed any fear I had of contracting HIV, the virus that causes AIDS. Everything I needed in needles and syringes was available to me on the Adolescent Unit. I chose the gauges I preferred for needles, snatched syringes and put them in my volunteer coat pocket. It felt like a very shameful thing to do, but I knew it was worth any feelings of shame I might have to avoid AIDS.

Shortly after I began working at the hospital, I was accepted into the Yale University Frontiers of Applied Science program, sponsored by the school of engineering. It consisted of a series of lectures and lab tours. I tried to be enthusiastic about it, but it was held on Saturday mornings. After partying all Friday night, it was hard to wake up and go to a lecture on Saturday morning.

The first lecture was held on the weekend that we had the winter Sea Explorers camping trip, and I chose not to attend the lecture. My grandparents were going away for the week, and they let me take their truck up to Sequassen. In the truck box I carried two cases of Heineken. I followed Al and Mark, who took Al's truck. We got up there three hours earlier than everyone else. The ranger wouldn't open the cabin for us because Mr. Holm hadn't arrived yet. So we drove across the street to another section of the camp. Then Al and I drove back to the main parking lot, but Mark drove Al's truck along the camp's back roads. About twenty minutes later, while Al and I were having a beer, Mark came running down the road. He'd driven Al's truck down a trail and got it stuck in ice. We went to try to get it out, but we couldn't.

It was getting dark, and it was half raining, half snowing. Mark and I took my truck and drove into town to get a tow truck. By the time we got Al's truck out, he was pretty crocked. He went with me to get my sleeping bag from my aunt Bonni's new house in Watertown. Bonni was getting ready to eat dinner. We were starving, so we ate with Bonni and a couple of her friends. But I was pretty anxious to get back to camp so that I could drink. I had to drive quite a bit, so I hadn't been drinking much at all. I had had two beers that day.

When we got back to camp I was all stressed out because on the highway there had been an avalanche or something, so there was a line of traffic for miles. At the camp one of the adult leaders bitched at us for leaving without permission. We didn't care. I told her that since no one else had arrived when we left we weren't going to wait for permission. At my first opportunity I started drinking. Later on that night we all sat on the front porch of the dining hall and drank beers. I couldn't imagine going on those trips and staying sober. We always brought some kind of drug or alcohol. The next day everyone went skiing, but Al and I stayed behind with a couple of others at the camp. We drank all day.

That evening, Mark took one of my Elavils and proceeded to pass out for about 12 hours. I think that Mr. Holm knew Mark had taken something because he asked me if there was something wrong with him. It wasn't hard to piece together. Before we left to go home on Sunday, we had to sneak the remaining beer back into my truck. The hard part was getting it past Mr. Holm. Al and Mark snuck it up a hill, and I locked it in the box. But later Mr. Holm wanted me to open the box and put a bag of his inside it. He was probably suspicious because I wouldn't open it, but I didn't care. When we got home, Al and I stopped at the boat works to hide the beer in the ship's locker. No one ever looked in there during the winter.

On my 17th birthday I got a car. My mother gave me her Z-28, a five-speed with a 305 V-8 engine. I was so excited. I had wanted that car since eighth grade. My mother bought a new

Camaro because we thought the Z-28's engine was dead. It ended up being a minor problem, so I got it for my birthday. I was very happy. Now I could go get my drugs whenever I wanted to. I didn't have to wait until I could borrow a car from my parents.

In March I had my first experience with a patient dying at Yale. It was a 12-year-old boy who had acute myeloblastic leukemia. He died only four months after he was diagnosed. It was very sad. That was one of the factors in my decision that I really wanted to become an oncologist. I had a strong desire to cure cancer, or at least make cancer patients' lives more livable. Seeing the deterioration of this boy and watching him suffer was very difficult for me. When he finally died I felt that maybe he was better off, because living had become too painful for him.

Shortly after he died, another boy died after being in remission for five years. After that I never again had the desire to commit suicide. I didn't think it was funny to joke around about death anymore. I realized that life ending was not funny. I didn't want to stop using drugs, but I didn't want to die.

In late April, Al and I tried to grow pot. I bought the magazine *High Times* for marijuana lovers. We bought Miracle-Gro and tried to turn my porch into a greenhouse. It was the sunniest place in the house, so we set up little cartons with soil in them and tried it. It didn't work, though. Every day Al and I rushed to my house after school to check and see if there was a sprout. After a month or so we gave up.

I was drinking more than I had been in a while. I still kept a bottle of Jack Daniel's in my closet. I wrote in my journal, "I hope the people in the Ship don't think that Al and I don't drink, because we do. It isn't like we're alcoholics or anything." I was trying very hard only to smoke pot and drink. Even though I didn't want to continue to do cocaine, I always kept some around.

On May 16 I totaled my car. I was driving to school and a man in a white van made an illegal left turn and hit me. I jumped out of my car and ran over to him, screaming at him. Then I ran into a store and called the police and my mother. My mother got there first. The cop gave the guy a ticket, and then I saw an old man talking to the cop, telling him that I was probably going too fast because I was a teenager. He's lucky I didn't go and kill him.

I cried all that day. I was really depressed because that car was very special to me. The accident was my excuse to get high. That afternoon I drank until I passed out, and that night I did cocaine until my nose bled. I was so upset over the whole thing that I didn't go to school that day or the next.

My parents were going to Florida the last week in May for five days. I was looking forward to it. My 23-year-old uncle and his girlfriend were going to stay with me.

The day after my parents left was skip day, and I didn't go to school. That night I volunteered on the Adolescent Unit for the last time, and then I had a party. I had a case of beer for me, about four joints, and coke. I shared the pot and some of the beer in the end, but not my cocaine. My uncle was surprised when I smoked the bowl that was being passed around. Because of Drug Free Milford, he thought that I had stopped doing drugs. He knew that I'd smoked pot at one time but didn't know that I still did.

That night was crazy for me. It was like I was looking to break records for how much I could use in one evening. I started out drinking beer, then beer and Jack Daniel's. Then I smoked a bowl, then a few joints. Then I went up to my room and did some blow. I called Jill and I could barely stand up to talk to her. I called Mark at work, and I was slurring my words, telling him that I was drunk, as if he couldn't tell. I don't remember anything that happened after about 10:30 because I had a blackout. I woke up the next morning fully dressed. It was the morning of my College Board Achievement Tests. I had to take three of them: English, chemistry, and math. I felt very sick. I drove Brooke, who was taking her SATs that day. I left after the first two tests because I felt too sick to continue. I sat out in the car for an hour waiting for Brooke to finish.

That Tuesday I spoke to a group for the first time about my personal experiences with drugs and alcohol. It was to a class of graduate students that Dave Ullman taught at a local university. It was funny in a way because I was supposed to talk about how I used to do drugs, but I didn't anymore, and tell them how I'd stopped. I went and gave them a few stories about housing projects and dealers and made it sound like I had miraculously stopped using on my own, with no outside help at all.

I started a job at a local drugstore in June. I also started getting into some very strange moods. I would get stoned after school and ponder my life. I wrote a lot in my journal. Here are a few entries :

June 13, 1990
I have a myriad of emotions I need to sort out. I'm pretty confused. My Chemistry teacher gave me a warning notice that I'm in danger of failing for the year. I wonder why my life is so damn difficult? I wish I could just do my high school years over again. In fact, how about starting at about ten years old? That's about when everything started to get screwed up. My adolescence is the modern example of the "domino theory." Nothing ever goes right once something goes wrong.

June 14, 1990
I started losing control in school. Slowly I could feel my anxiety and blood pressure rising. There's a strange feeling I get in my stomach. I know it, although it's only happened three or four other times in my life. I'm not sure what I would do if I didn't have any friends. I'm a little surprised that I never killed myself. I feel like I'm living in a permanent ambivalence about drugs. In a way I want to keep using, and in another way I want to stop. I don't want to use cocaine with the excuse that I'm depressed. I need a car.

June 17, 1990
I need someone who can help me get some control over my life. I need something with substance in my life. If not I don't know what I'll do. At least I got a car.

June 18, 1990
I was sent home today for being suicidal. That certainly isn't my problem. Drugs are. I'm not pissed or anything, though. I still can't believe it happened. Pretty fucked up. And Saturday night I just got through telling Jill that this was the first year that I haven't gotten sent home. Guess I spoke too soon. Could've been worse. It was the last day of classes, too, not even a full day. I think they overreacted. My father hasn't said one thing about it. I'm glad. I don't want to hear it.

June 23, 1990
I don't understand why sometimes it seems impossible to make it through the day. It scares me when I feel so

bad at night that I wonder if I'm even going to wake up the next morning. I don't think I'd call myself suicidal. I believe I'm a realist. I don't care if people around me think I set my goals too high. If you're not willing to reach for something beyond what is "safe" why bother trying at all? You might as well give up right there and die because you're no longer serving a purpose.

There is no question about the fact that drugs ruin lives. Once you use them regularly you're never the same. The innocence in your life is gone, and you just can't get that back. I wish I had never seen a drug in my life.

A week after the end of my junior year I started working for the Comprehensive Cancer Center at Yale. It felt really good to be introduced as a volunteer who has done "a tremendous amount of work at Yale-New Haven Hospital." I was the first volunteer to work at the cancer center. I decided that I didn't want cocaine to be a part of my life anymore.

I abstained for a record 18 days. It was hellish because all I thought about was cocaine, every minute of the day. I couldn't stand obsessing over the drug like that. I finally decided that it was easier to use than to keep away from it. No one knew what I was doing. It was my own secret. I put my using out of my mind. I stopped analyzing it. It was like I was using, but I wouldn't admit it to myself. Somehow I kept it a secret from everybody, even myself.

CHAPTER SIX

During July I started analyzing my mind. I wondered why I felt the way I was feeling. In my journal I found myself wishing I could understand who I was. Was I the type who'd be a doctor and a success, or a depressed drug addict? I didn't know. I figured I fell somewhere in between.

I remembered back to when I first started seeing the school psychologist in middle school, and traced back what had happened to me. I thought about all the times I had thought about and halfheartedly tried suicide. I wanted to know what my motives had been. I'd believed it was up to the individual to decide the direction of his or her life and whether or not to continue or end it. I hadn't intended to kill myself. It was just important to know that I always had options.

Al was going to college in late August. I knew I'd miss him. Along with being a little depressed about Al going away, I was sad that Zack wasn't using anymore. I had to look for cocaine myself. I hated that. Sometimes I was desperate enough to go to housing projects in Bridgeport and New Haven to get my cocaine. I was at the point where I didn't care what I had to do. I needed the drug too much to be careful about how I got it.

I got burned for the first time one night in Father Panik Village, a project in Bridgeport. I lost $50. The dealer took the money for my coke and left. I wasn't upset about losing the money. I was pissed that I got shorted on my coke.

The next week I went to a crack house in New Haven with Rich, an old friend from middle school. It was an old house that had probably been very nice at one time, but now it was dilapidated and broken-down. Outside in the yard there were empty vials scattered around. Inside it smelled like crack and a mixture of dirty people and rotting food. The floor was covered with so much garbage it was hard to walk around. Everytime I kicked something out of my way, roaches would scatter from under it. It was making me sick. The three guys living there looked like they hadn't showered in years and they smelled that way, too. There was little furniture, and at first I had no interest in sitting on it anyway. In my mind I was kicking myself for not getting ripped before going. Rich made himself right at home. At first, everything was okay, the three guys seemed nice enough. We were going to freebase, because they didn't smoke crack. They only made it. First we snorted, and I felt more comfortable. I sat down on the couch and tried to forget about how gross the place was. One of the guys who was cooking crack in the kitchen was paranoid about me being there. After a little while, he came out and put a gun to my head. He was asking me if I was a cop.

I was afraid to move for fear that he'd shoot me. Rich screamed at him, "She isn't a bust! Put the fucking gun down." The guy put it down and laughed. He apologized and offered to let me have the first hit off the pipe. That was good enough for me. Once we started basing, the seaminess of the place didn't bother me. I began to enjoy myself. I had always preferred freebasing to line cocaine. I just didn't get the chance to do it that often.

I blacked out several times over the summer. I was really into drinking alone, especially Jack Daniel's, still my favorite beverage. On many occasions I couldn't remember blocks of time from the day before. I was seriously questioning if I might have a drug problem.

I was also thinking about college and where I wanted to go. At the end of August I made a tentative list of where I wanted to apply. All of the schools were out West, far from home. I was trying to straighten myself out. I knew that I would have to work very hard senior year if I wanted to get into a college that I liked. Because of my poor academic record, Tulane was no longer a very realistic option, and I looked into schools that I was more likely to get into.

I was still involved with my work at the hospital and the cancer center. On August 16 I went to a local camp for kids with cancer.

On August 18 I was supposed to go to a birthday party for someone I'd gone to Lauralton with. I was about to call to say I couldn't make it when she called me. It was going to be at the house of another girl that was in our class. The girl whose birthday it was, Sue, said I wasn't allowed to go because the parents of the girl having the party didn't want me in their house. I thought it was pretty funny, but my friends felt bad because they hadn't wanted to hurt my feelings. I was used to it, though, because throughout my life many friends' parents had forbidden me to be with their children.

Al and Mark came over to my house one day with two girls from the Ship, Stacy and Leslie. Al got drunk. While I was upstairs, he and Mark got into a fight. I heard this loud banging, and the next thing I knew Al was running up the stairs.

Mark had punched him in the mouth. To keep them from fighting further, we left Al at my house and took a ride to the cemetery to see Chuck's grave. We had a picnic there. It was morbid but nice. When we got back to my house about an hour and a half later, Al was really crocked. He was on the phone with Keri. I wanted to get drunk, too, because it just wasn't possible for me to watch someone else use and not do it myself. At least I took Stacy and Leslie home first. They didn't need to watch.

By the end of August I began to suspect that I had a drug problem. But I didn't think I could get help even if I wanted to. What would people say? I couldn't allow something like that to come out. It had been bothering me that people were telling me how well I was doing when I knew that there was a part of my life that no one knew about. I wasn't doing anything to even try to stop using. I was afraid to. I feared that when I tried to stop I wouldn't be able to and would have to admit that I was an addict and alcoholic.

I was really looking forward to senior year. It was going to be great. I was sure of that. I was going to have a good time, and there was no way anyone was going to tell me different.

A lot of kids were leaving from Sea Explorers to go to college. I had never been an officer, so I decided that since it was my last year in the Ship, I would run for president, which they call boatswain. No one ran against anyone running for office. I was boatswain, and Mark was boatswain's mate. It was really cool because we were best friends and the head officers.

I couldn't go anywhere without using. There was a time when I wouldn't use around certain people, such as people in the Ship. But there was an instance just before school started when I did. Keri went out with Jill and me. We also took Jay and Mike, two of my using friends. Jill didn't use, but she still hung out with us. After I'd finally dropped off the last person,

I was so stoned that I went to go home on Interstate 95 but got on the wrong way. I didn't realize it until I was 20 miles south of Milford. I thought it was funny. I laughed the whole way home.

When school started, I finished working at the cancer center. I got a certificate for volunteering and signed up for emergency-room training because that was where I wanted to work next. On the first day of September I got drunk to celebrate senior year. I missed Al a lot (he had gone away to school in New York), but I was using enough for the both of us. Every day I was making the drive up to New Haven to buy cocaine.

CHAPTER
SEVEN
▼

In September of my senior year things changed for me a lot. I found myself feeling guilty because I respected Dave Ullman and didn't want him to know that I was still doing drugs and drinking. After some consideration I decided to tell him that my summer had been less than drug free. It was difficult to tell him, but I finally confessed that I was still using cocaine and had been the entire time I'd known him. He suggested that I join a support group that was held at Foran High School every Friday. I was open to the idea, and on September 14 I met Pat McDonough, the counselor who ran the group. He said I definitely met the criteria for his "psychoeducational" group.

But that didn't stop me from wanting to get high. On one hand, I was afraid of landing in rehab. On the other, I was sure I didn't have a problem. I was in classic denial. I was looking forward to group because I was expecting to see that everybody else was ten times worse than I was. I figured that I'd be with people that made my drug use look like nothing. I was also hoping to maybe get a couple new coke buddies. I assumed that I wouldn't be the only one who was a regular user of cocaine. After my first group meeting, this is what I wrote:

> *I had my first drug group meeting this morning. It was cool. Kris was the only person I knew. He sold me a dose of LSD during lunch. Everyone in it is still using, I think. Kris and I are going to Bridgeport on Monday to buy some crack, probably because I'm jonesin' bad. It's been four days since I last did coke. I need to get high. I'm in need of a rush. If anyone ever read this I'd keel over and die. None of my friends know I'm like this.*

Pat's first impression of me was that of a sad, confused, and unhappy kid. He could tell that I was sensitive, although I tried to cover that up with a tough-guy act. He recognized that I was using my intelligence as a defense mechanism. Instead of feeling things in my heart, I would analyze them in my mind first. That reduced the amount of emotions that I actually had to feel. Pat saw me as searching for someone to help me, to listen to and support me. He immediately saw my cocaine habit as a serious problem because of my self-destructive use patterns.

My parents went on a cruise the day after my first group. The next day Kate came over and we went into New Haven to buy. I had been working for several months and I still had nothing to show for it. However I was supporting my own drug habit for the most part and wasn't stealing anymore. That day I only had $70, so I couldn't get much. I got a little more than a gram. We bought it from a kid we didn't even know. We did a few lines before I dropped Kate off and went home. I tried to control myself, but I ended up doing the rest pretty quickly. I collected money from someone who owed me and I got more cash at the bank with my ATM card. I drove back to New Haven and bought an eight ball, 3.5 grams. I told myself that this time I would stretch it out and not do it all at once. I was proud of myself because I managed to spread it out over two days. I got high before I went to see Bob, my therapist. I was having a great time without my parents around. I was driving my mother's car, which was cool.

That week I also gave Mark his first line of cocaine. When I got home from seeing Bob I was in possession of some more coke. I took a shower because I felt sick from having cold sweats. When I was drying my hair, Mark came upstairs. I set out a mirror. He did one line and I did six. I felt guilty about giving him coke, but I justified it by saying that it was only one line. But two days later, I gave him two more lines. This is what I wrote September 26, about what was going on with the coke and Mark: "Well, I don't know what to say for myself. I feel kind of bad, and I kind of don't. Actually, I don't really care."

At school a girl in the group had been talking about Narcotics Anonymous (NA). I didn't know anything about NA. I thought it was only for heroin addicts. She said that it wasn't like that at all. I assumed then that she must have been seriously into cocaine to be in NA. I didn't know anything about her, but she seemed really serious about helping us in the group in any way she could. I told her I was interested in going to a meeting sometime. She gave me her number and the address of the meeting held in Milford on Monday nights. After that I considered going to a meeting. I was also interested in Cocaine Anonymous, but my denial told me that I wasn't bad enough yet, that I still had no problem at all.

Right after that I talked to Tricia for the first time in a while. My parents were still away. She wanted to do some coke with me. I didn't want to share what I had, but I was more than willing to get some more with her. But she was backing out on me. It was because she didn't want to spend her money on coke. Her parents definitely would've wanted to know where her money had gone. So instead of going with her, I went with this guy Mike to get coke in New Haven, the day before my parents were coming home.

It was the morning that I was going on a sailing trip with Sea Explorers. We went all over New Haven looking for coke, trying several sources, people that we knew and trusted. No one was around. I was getting nervous because I needed to get coke that day and I wasn't going to give up until I got it. I drove us to a project. It wasn't that dangerous a place or anything. It was pretty calm. Two kids, 17 or 18 years old, were selling. They walked up to the car when I pulled up. I gave one of them the money and said I wanted an eight ball. After he handed over the coke, I started to pull away. The bigger of the two pulled out a pistol and told Mike and me to get out of the car. I said, "Fuck you, you'll have to shoot me if you want me to get out." Mike punched me on the arm and got out of the car. He walked over to the kid and talked to him, trying to calm him down. The other kid laughed and pulled the gun away. He said that his brother was new at dealing and wasn't used to selling to "rich kids" yet. He thought I was a bust. So I did a couple lines with them to show them it was cool. I guess that experience would've scared a normal person, but I didn't mind at all. The only thing that mattered to me was getting my cocaine.

Now that I look back I see that I really would've done anything for cocaine. There were no limits to what I would do to get high. If I thought I could get coke for it, I'd have cut off a finger, or my whole hand if necessary. My mind was constantly on cocaine. In Physics, when we used weights in lab, I would relate to my friends how much money it would cost to buy that weight in coke. Sometimes I thought I would spend my whole life with the one-track desire to get high. I couldn't understand why people were afraid of cocaine. None of my friends, other than Mark, would ever touch the drug. Those were my drinking friends. Before I tried the drug, I had been afraid to snort it, then I was afraid to smoke it, then afraid to shoot it. But I had quickly grown to enjoy every way of using cocaine.

My favorite way of using cocaine was intravenously. I felt that there was no better feeling than that of sticking a needle in my arm. As soon as I'd done it the first time, I knew that shooting coke was the best way to get high. If I was ever afraid of needles, you'd never know it by watching me shoot up. It was my most guarded secret though, because I knew I'd be in rehab in a heartbeat if anyone ever found out. I don't bruise when I get injections, or show any physical signs, and that helped me keep it a secret. I didn't get to shoot coke as often as I'd have liked, though, because the whole process was a little too conspicuous to do in my house.

For Mark's birthday in October we had a little party to celebrate. It was a Tuesday, before a Sea Explorers meeting. Mark and I went to Bridgeport with Jay to buy some liquor at a store that would serve us. We got a six-pack of beer, a bottle of Nightrain, and a fifth of 100 proof vodka. Then we went and picked up Mike and Nyla, Mike's girlfriend. We went to a park in Bridgeport and drank in the parking lot. I had a beer, some vodka, and some Nightrain but I wasn't drunk or anything. Mark was drinking really fast, and a lot, so he was trashed. Nyla and I walked up to a dam and smoked a couple of cigarettes and a joint. A couple minutes later we saw Jay and Mark walking on the rocks through the water. It was funny because you could tell that they were drunk by the way they stumbled over the rocks. Jay fell and was soaking wet. When we came down from the dam and went over to the car, Mike, Jay, and Mark were talking to a homeless couple living out of their car. Mike was leaning on the driver's-side back window, and when he moved, it shattered. We had given them a pack of cigarettes and a few cups of Nightrain so they weren't pissed at first. We left right away, though. I dropped Nyla off home.

Then we went to Jay's house so that he and Mike could get ready for night school. At Jay's house, Mark told me he felt sick, but I didn't think that he was actually going to vomit. As soon as we pulled up at the high school to drop off Mike and Jay, Mark puked out my car window. Mike and Jay left, and Mark did it again. I stopped at a gas station so that he could clean himself up before we picked up Jill. He threw up outside and inside the bathroom. I used the gas station squeegee to wash off the side of my car. When we got to Jill's house, Mark puked in the bushes in her driveway. I rang the bell and rushed Jill out to the car so that her parents wouldn't notice anything. I had to stop before we got on the parkway so that Mark could throw up again. I gave him a shirt to wear for the Sea Explorers meeting when we got to my house. We bought him a little bottle of water to drink when he felt better. He was okay for a while at the meeting. He sat on the floor with Jill, next to the garbage can. About 15 minutes into the meeting he took a sip of water and threw it up on the wall. He went outside and the Holms gave me a really dirty look because they suspected that he'd been drinking. I glanced over at Sara and started laughing. That really pissed them off. Mrs. Holm said, "It isn't funny, Chris." When the meeting was over Mr. Holm came up to me and asked me if Mark was drunk. I denied it, of course. They never forgot that incident, and Mark didn't drink again for some time.

After that I had to wonder about our status in the Ship. I thought that I had done the right thing by taking Mark to the meeting. I couldn't have taken him home to his parents. Not the way he was.

On October 4 I trained to become an emergency-room volunteer. Another kid and I were the only high school students working in the ER. I was really looking forward to it. That week, Dave Ullman called an Alateen sponsor and had me get in touch with her. In group, Pat McDonough said that soon they would be asking me for a commitment to stay clean at least one day a week. I thought it was going to be easy. I figured that I could do that, no problem. It would be the day that I was scheduled to work in the ER. I wasn't very interested in staying sober at all. I still didn't see any problem with my using. I laughed at my friends and said that I must be a functioning addict or alcoholic because I could still be in honors classes, apply to college, work, and volunteer while using as heavily as I was. It was making school and work unmanageable, but I just didn't see it at the time.

Also one day in early October Mark and I picked up Al from school. That night Al and I partied with four other kids. Jill stayed sober, and so did Al for the most part. The rest of us were trashed. By eleven o'clock, I could barely walk. We'd taken my car, and Al was the designated driver. By the time we got to my house I'd sobered up. I had a talent for getting sober as soon as I walked through my door.

The next day I had to go to work. I was working at a drugstore, but I left early because I was dizzy and dehydrated. My boss probably knew what was wrong with me. I told Mike, my friend who also worked there, that I had a hangover. We talked about what went on with me a lot at work, but I guess my boss didn't think we were serious. Later I split a bag of weed with Al, but I didn't use because I was still recovering from our little party. It was my first day clean in a little over a week.

I went to Alateen on October 8. It was interesting, but I can't remember exactly what went on. I do remember some of my feelings. I didn't feel that comfortable because I was still using and the other kids weren't. I was planning on going back, though. It felt like the right thing to do. On October 10 I called the Narcotics Anonymous hotline to see if there were any convenient meetings. There were, but I didn't go.

The next night I got home at 1:30 A.M. from making a bad coke deal. I should've known better than to go to the Father Panik Village again to buy. I only lost $30. It was probably better that way, but I was pissed that I didn't get all of my coke.

In group that morning I had been trying to be quiet and not say anything until my friend Kelly pointed out how they were forgetting me. She said that I was cool and all, but I was getting messed up. Then Pat McDonough asked me how it felt to hear that about myself. Everybody was telling me how they'd support me if I tried to quit. Pat told me to think about the Milford Mental Health Clinic. I said I didn't want to go there and asked him for another alternative. Then he told me I could consider inpatient treatment. But I didn't think I was that bad. I told them I had been straight all day Thursday, which I thought was 99 percent true because all I did was smoke half a joint to relax. I told the group I'd try three days clean the next week, but I knew there was no way I could do that.

I was under the impression that a day clean just meant no cocaine but that it was okay to drink and smoke pot. It wasn't that I didn't want to see what I was doing. I couldn't. It took months of people confronting me about my use before I began to admit that I needed help. There were times when I started thinking about rehab, but I put that thought out of my mind as soon as it entered. I didn't want to tell my parents. My lying to them was very involved. They had absolutely no idea of what was going on. I was very good at hiding what I was doing. No one knew unless I wanted them to know. Only a select number of people knew about my use, and there was never anybody who knew everything. Even though I was honest with a few people, I still kept things from them. Until recently I never admitted to my friends that I'd been using cocaine intravenously. That was the type of thing that I thought would get me sent to rehab if I admitted it. I didn't know of anyone my age who had done it, so no one could know I did.

CHAPTER

EIGHT
▼

On October 15, 1990, I went to my first Narcotics Anonymous meeting. It was at a church right down the street from my house. I'd been nervous with anticipation all day. I pulled into the parking lot and waited for a few minutes in my car. I felt like there was a ton of bricks on my chest as I opened the church door. As I walked down the stairs to the basement, my heart was racing. I felt relieved to see Rachel, my friend from group, in the room where the meeting was held. There seemed to be a million people there. I took a seat next to Rachel and thanked God it was a smoking meeting. I had a feeling I'd be smoking quite a bit that night.

Shortly after I arrived the chairman introduced himself as an addict and asked for some readings. There were five readings: "Who Is an Addict?," "What Is the Narcotics Anonymous Program?," "Why Are We Here?," "How It Works (the Twelve Steps)," and "The Twelve Traditions of NA." After that the man asked if anyone was attending their first NA meeting. I raised my hand and was welcomed. Then he asked if anyone wanted to recognize any clean time. People raised their hands if they happened to be on a significant anniversary of sobriety. It was a "Recovery Text" meeting, so one of the stories in the NA text was read next. Each person read a paragraph until the story was finished.

When the story had been read, the lights were turned off and candles were lit. I found it a very relaxing atmosphere. I sat back and listened intently to addicts sharing their feelings about the story and anything else they wanted to talk about. I couldn't believe how much I related to what was being said. In my head I was trying to deal with the reality that I might be an addict. Every moment it was becoming more apparent that, yes, I did belong in that room.

About 45 minutes into the meeting there was a coffee break. I went outside to get some air and collect my thoughts. I talked to Rachel about what I was thinking. I wanted to keep coming back. For the first time in a while I saw a light at the end of my tunnel. I saw that this fellowship might actually be the way for me to salvage my life. Finally there was hope. When the meeting began again I listened to more people, and when it was over I didn't want to leave. Rachel collected a pile of literature for me and a Connecticut meeting schedule. I made a commitment to myself to give this program a chance and return. I couldn't wait to have what everyone else there seemed to have—freedom from the pain of active addiction.

Two days later I smoked a joint with my mother for the first time. I'd always wanted to do that. We were driving home from the Trumbull mall. She lit up and asked me if I wanted some. We didn't talk much at all. We did talk a little about our upcoming trip to California and Arizona. It was a bonding experience. I was excited. I felt bad, though. She didn't know that I had a problem with drugs. If she'd known about the extent of my problem, she never would've smoked with me. I guess she figured it was okay because I was 17 and capable of making my own decision about it.

The next day a kid called me to ask for weed. It made me feel like a drug dealer. And then he referred to me as a "major stoner." That made me do a lot of thinking. Why was I killing myself with drugs? Probably because drugs were the only way of life I knew. I felt my best after doing some lines or getting baked or drunk. It wasn't ruining my life. I had a job. I volunteered at a hospital. My grades were fine. It didn't seem to me like I had a problem. But I spent all my money on drugs, and when I started to run low, I began thinking of ways to get the money I needed to buy enough to support my habit. I needed to get high all the time because I felt like shit when I wasn't. My friends were concerned over my use, but I figured it was my life and I could do what I wanted. I thought I could stop the next day if I felt like it, which, of course, I didn't.

That Friday at group, proud of myself for staying clean for three days, and only doing coke once, I admitted to Pat McDonough and the group that I had a drug problem. The meeting lasted for an hour and a half. Pat asked me what I was going to do about my problem. I didn't really know.

That Saturday at a Sea Explorers hayride, I told the Holms that I was an addict. They told me it felt like a slap in the face, that they were hurt and disappointed, and they didn't have the patience to help me through this. They didn't feel comfortable around me anymore, but I was glad that I'd finally told them. Mrs. Holm said they'd never be able to trust me again because once I'd looked her straight in the face and said I wasn't using. Actually, I wasn't too thrilled with what they had to say. I expected them to be disappointed but not to take it so personally.

What the Holms didn't know was that I'd already gotten stoned when I told them I was an addict. Al and I got baked in my car in a restaurant parking lot before we got to the hayride.

We finished smoking a joint and opened the car doors to get out. A huge cloud of pot smoke drifted out. A couple walking by us started chuckling. Jill and a few people from the Ship walked over to the car and started laughing. Al and I hadn't realized how badly it smelled like pot around my car. After the hayride, everyone sat around a bonfire and hung out before going home. Al, Jill, and I went to my car so Al and I could get stoned again. When we were through, and Jill and I were going back to the bonfire, Mr. Holm stopped me. He told me that he thought I was too intelligent to get so mixed up in drugs. It seemed so ironic that I was stoned while admitting my addiction. I probably should've felt guilty or ashamed, but I didn't think I'd done anything wrong that night.

I was making a lot of friends at school because people really wanted me to stay clean. I was overwhelmed by the support I got. In my journal on October 26 I wrote that everybody in group was happy for me because I had used coke only twice since the week before and had gone four days clean. Most people that were partying didn't want me to use with them because they knew I had a problem. Many people who didn't use were very interested in hearing about what it was like. I was enjoying myself at Foran. I felt like I belonged there. I was glad that I left Lauralton.

In November my mother and I went to California and Arizona to look at colleges. It was a really cool trip. I liked all the schools we saw, but I especially liked Arizona State University and UCLA. I knew that ASU was the only realistic choice of the two. We came home on November 14, and I wasted no time. On November 15 I was using again. I was going to NA once a week, but it wasn't enough to help me stay clean. Jill's ex-boyfriend said he was going to get me some coke, and I was excited about that. I went to a keg party and got really drunk and stoned after thinking about it all day. But I didn't do any cocaine that day so I didn't think that what I was doing was bad. During school when I told him I was going to a party that night, Dave Ullman got pissed and told me to leave my friends in a cesspool someday. At the party I drank until I could hardly walk. I thought it was funny.

Around that time this is what I wrote in my journal:

It's really hard for me to believe that I really am a drug addict. But I guess it's true that I will continue using until I die if I don't stop and stay clean. It's so hard. I feel like I need it as much as I need to breathe. Today I was able to stay clean. But I probably won't stay clean tomorrow.

During group at the end of November I started talking about how I wouldn't mind if I died. Pat McDonough got concerned and talked to me about it after group. He said I had to go to Milford Mental Health once a week. He wanted me to call for an appointment for an evaluation. I really didn't want to go to another counselor. It was just another person to tell me that I was messed up. I really was afraid they would send me to rehab.

My denial was so deep that I never realized that what I was doing was so destructive. People were pointing out that I was getting worse. Whenever someone tried to confront me about my use, I'd completely deny that I might have a problem. Even though I knew I did, I just couldn't admit it out loud to people who weren't in NA. There were so many people telling me that I was messed up—Dave, Pat, the kids in group with me. It really made me think. Although I had been consciously questioning myself since ninth grade, I thought it had been normal for me to progress to cocaine use. I really didn't think that I was that bad. I felt as if I was immune to addiction because of my intelligence and promising future. I kept asking my friends if they thought I really honestly had a problem. I tried to believe I could quit any time I wanted to, that I just wasn't ready yet. Even though I knew that willpower had nothing to do with addiction, I considered myself a strong person. I had convinced myself that I was in control of my life. I was blocking out the insanity around me and ignoring all the problems that were caused by drugs. Not many people actually came out and told me that I was messed up. But Pat did. I respected that. I knew that he wasn't screwing around. But it didn't matter what people said to me. I needed to make the decision to change for myself.

It was in December that people started seriously confronting me about my use and my inability to stop using. I was getting to be really good friends with the kids in group. I respected what they said to me. I'd had the wrong impression before I went into group in September. They weren't worse than I was. I was screwed up compared to most of them. That was what I needed to see. I loved Foran and continued to thank God that I had been kicked out of Lauralton. I knew I might have been dead if I hadn't.

December 5, 1990
I called Greg Ryan at Milford Mental Health today. In a way, I want to go, but in another way I don't. Will I ever feel normal again? Did I ever? I wish I had some coke. I'm craving bad. I'm so depressed. I have to refill my Elavil tonight. I think I should take the whole bottle while sitting in some deserted spot. And sooner or later someone will find me dead. If anyone ever heard me talking like this I'd be in the psych ward of a hospital within a couple hours.

That night, Mr. Holm called me to say that Mark and I were indefinitely suspended from the Ship. He said we talked about drugs too much and were a bad influence on his daughter and the younger kids. I got really pissed off but stayed calm. I knew I had to start being honest about everything. I told my mother about that and about Milford Mental Health. I didn't really care about leaving the Ship. What bothered me was that he had kicked us out. I didn't think he could just make us leave because he didn't want us there. We were in America. I could talk about whatever I felt like. Stacy and Leslie from the Ship both agreed that it was ridiculous to say that we talked about drugs too much. My parents wanted to call and tell the Holms off, but I asked them not to. I didn't want to bring them into it. Mark couldn't tell his parents because they wouldn't understand. They'd be pissed at him. I felt bad because I knew that Mark wouldn't be accused of being a bad influence if it wasn't for me. Then I found out that Mr. Holm actually told Mark that I was a bad influence on him and it was because of me that this happened. He said that Mark and I might as well be the kids' "pushers." That made me furious. There's no way that Mark and I would've ever tried to get anyone else in the Ship involved with drugs or alcohol. I always gave the younger kids a message that was clearly anti-drug. They never saw me use and I never told them that I was involved with drugs. The worst that they ever saw me do was smoke cigarettes.

I wrote a letter to Art Lobdell, the Boy Scouts' district executive, explaining to him what had happened. He knew Mark and me, so I knew that he'd be able to tell us what we should do.

Just when things were looking bad, they got worse. On December 10, my friend Krisha got busted by security for stealing at the drugstore where I worked. That was all it took for me to get very paranoid. I was sure that they were going to get me the next time I went to work. I'd stolen from the store before to get cigarettes and things that I could sell or trade for drugs. I started going to work very high. I wanted to be able to tell the security people off if they came in to get me. I'd get really high and do all the coke I could on the way to work. Then I'd sweat and shake during work because I was craving. But the security people never came in for me, and everything was fine.

I finally made an appointment to see Greg Ryan at Milford Mental Health. I talked to Mr. Kosh, the vice principal, because I had to leave school to see Greg. I wanted to go without having a note from my parents. He said that since I was trying to do something to help myself, we could work something out. It made me feel better that he was such a nice guy and understood how I felt about the situation. I wasn't dreading my appointment with Greg anymore.

> *December 14, 1990*
> *I just got home from Josh's party. I'm drunk. I had fun. Today in group Pat told me to seriously consider inpatient rehab. Dave made me go to the nurse. They called down Mr. Kosh. I was talking to him about coke. Now he knows, too. It was a screwed-up day. Art Lobdell called. Mark and I are meeting with him Monday to talk about leaving the Ship.*

> *December 17, 1990*
> *At this point I want to stop using. I've had enough. That's easy to say, but I can't do it. Especially when it's so easy to use. Mr. Dodd, my art teacher, told me today that he heard something very good about me at the Student Assistance Team meeting, that I was a big*

help to someone. I doubt it. How can I possibly be of help to anyone? I can't even help myself.

December 21, 1990
I had group today. Pat said I was messed-up (again). Kelly was getting upset because I laugh over my problem and it isn't funny. I picked up Al after school, and he stayed at my house while I saw Greg Ryan for the first time. He seems like a nice guy. I think I convinced him that I'm not suicidal and that I am happy. I wasn't lying; I am happy. There is no reason for him to get nervous about me.

December 22, 1990
I just got off the phone with Al. I think he's an alcoholic. I don't want to see him get any worse.

Pat had been frustrated and disappointed that I hadn't decided to go to treatment right away, and was fighting for me to go. He was pissed that we had to go through Milford Mental Health now. He could see that I didn't have much time left, that my life was in danger.

Christmas was nice. It would have been better if I had been in a more stable state of mind. I was trying to stay clean, but it was very frustrating. I managed to abstain from using for most of my school vacation. But I used on New Year's Eve and after that I kept using. I lied about staying clean. I hadn't done cocaine for a number of days, so I counted the last day I did coke as my clean date. It was pretty ridiculous.

My journal entries provide the best insight into what was going on with me during the month of January:

January 4, 1991
I have to see the psychiatrist at the Milford Mental Health Clinic at 8:15 in the morning on Tuesday. Greg said all clients have to get evaluated at least once. Great. I'm so sick of evaluations—will this ever end?

January 6, 1991
I didn't do very much today. I wished for cocaine. J. J. came over tonight (from the Ship). He told me that Mr. Holm told the Ship that we (Mark and I) are on drugs. That's the second time he's done that. It really pisses me off.

January 8, 1991
This morning I went to the psychiatrist at the clinic. She was nice. She said I need a complete blood count and an EKG. She says I have blunted emotions from the drugs. She told me to raise my Elavil dose from 75 mg. to 125 mg. She wants to treat my depression along with my headaches. Dave was really pissed when I told him. He said that you don't help people get off drugs by giving them more of another one. Mark and Al came over after school. Mark and I snorted No Doz. I've been jonesin' for coke bad and it was just an urge. Dave was also getting pissed at me today for calling myself a loser. I know that I'm not, but I feel that way sometimes.

My mother totally agreed with what the doctor said today about raising the Elavil and going for the EKG. I'm pretty ambivalent about the whole situation myself.

January 9, 1991
Kelly said that when she was talking to Dave this morning he said, "Chris does have some straight friends, you know." Whatever that's supposed to mean. I was telling Dave how he should try coke, and maybe he'd change his mind about it. Everyone should try it at least once.

January 11, 1991
I got accepted to Arizona State University today. I'm really excited. Pat announced in group today that he's leaving, and he'll only be at two more meetings at the most. He yelled at me for some time today, about how I need intensive treatment. He said I'm destroying myself with my anger. He told me that I have a special relationship with him and it's hurting me to lose that. It is *hurting me to lose him. I trust Pat, he is a real person, not some asshole who thinks they know about drugs. He's afraid I'm going to die, and I don't blame him. I'm not sure how our relationship got so special, but it did. He is the first person I ever got honest with. I was very desperate for coke today, and I was wiping mirrors and inhaling deeply into my grinder to get more. I even stuck Q-Tips into my vials to try to get high.*

January 12, 1991
I got very stoned tonight, and I'm feeling guilty. Should I lie in school Monday and keep telling people that I have 25 days clean? It isn't like I did coke or anything. It could've been much worse. I can't stand lying like this, but I'm trying to protect myself. I don't want people to be concerned about me. I'll be fine. I wish I hadn't smoked pot today. I wonder what it

would be like if I had six months or a year clean? Will I ever know? It's so hard. I need to change my attitudes about everything. I can't believe I got into ASU. I think I'm going to go there. It takes a lot of pressure off me. I cannot believe how stoned I was today. But I really want coke. Screw other drugs, there's only one that I truly enjoy.

January 13, 1991
I'm going to lie in school tomorrow and tell everyone I have 25 days clean. In fact, I plan to keep lying like that. Hey, at least I didn't use today.

January 14, 1991
Well, I used today, but I don't plan on telling anyone. I lied to Dave today and told him that I have 25 days clean, and tomorrow it'll be 26. I don't feel like hearing everyone's shit, so I'll lie and no one will bother me. I feel guilty, though. I wish Pat wasn't leaving. I don't want to get to know someone new. I'm really thinking a lot about next year. I think I'm gonna commit to ASU.

January 15, 1991
I pointed a loaded gun at my head and in my mouth today. It really freaked everyone out. It was nothing. I was just screwing around. I think I'm going to Stamford with Kelly and maybe Pete Saturday. Hopefully we'll get tanked.

January 16, 1991
Greg told me I should go to inpatient today, because I don't know how to have fun without drugs. He also

said his usual—I build up a defensive wall and I don't let people get close to me. Greg is right about me so far. He said I have a great personality and there's something very likable about me. That's good. He also said that there's two people in me, the good kid and the drug addict.

January 17, 1991
I had an interesting day today. I told Dave about the gun thing, and of course he got all nervous and did his little intervention. During lunch he told me I need a 30–45 day inpatient program. There's something I haven't heard before! Then I got called down at the end of the day, and he was waiting for me outside the office. He had my guidance counselor call my mother. I told my mom what I did and proceeded to call Dave every name in the book. I was extremely pissed. Mrs. Brandon, a member of the Student Assistance Team, was down in the guidance office, and as a member of the team she got in on it. She goes, "We're only doing this because we love you, Chris." Well, what are they trying to accomplish by getting my parents involved? I don't need this shit. Pat should get a kick out of this situation. Tomorrow I'm saying that I have a month clean. I don't know why they overreacted so badly. I am far from suicidal. If I wanted to kill myself, I would've pulled the trigger. I knew that I shouldn't have said anything. They had better not mention drugs or rehab to my mother.

January 18, 1991
Well, so much happened today that I don't know where to start. I got to school at the regular time, but I

didn't go to homeroom. I warned Dave not to tell my mother about NA, that I would tell her when I was ready. My friend Margo witnessed our conversation. Then I went down to the office, and my mom was waiting for her meeting with Dave. Dave cancelled his first class to do it. I went to Physics late without a pass and sat there all nervous. Group was at 8:30 this morning. I got to the meeting early and Tara and I went to have a cigarette. We went back up a few minutes later, but Pat and Chris Burke, the new counselor, weren't there yet. So I let off some steam and told everyone what was going on. Pat said he wanted to talk to my mother. He wanted me to go to the Adolescent Crisis Unit for Treatment and Evaluation. My mother was gone by the time group was over. He said that Mr. Kosh had told him I was pissed at Ullman. Then we discussed my issue for a while. Chris Burke said, "I know I just met you, but I've seen a lot of kids like you, and they're all dead now." We talked about me going to rehab as usual. My mother's meeting lasted 45 minutes. I went to Dave to see what had happened. He said that it had gone well and that he suggested to my mother that I go to inpatient treatment. He also said that she said she'd think about it. I apologized for being so mean to him. I worked tonight until nine and then Mark and I discussed it with my mother for a while. The good news is that she has no intention of sending me to rehab. They were telling her that she shouldn't be sending me to Arizona, but she handled it well. They think I'm a danger to myself. Now I hope Dave, Pat, and Greg get off my back about the rehab issue. They wonder why I don't let people get close to me. When I

*do they end up screwing me over. I don't need anyone.
In seven months I'll be gone. I want to go and get
drunk and high tomorrow. I lied and told everyone I
have a month clean today. As if I could ever get a
month! They'll never know the difference.*

January 19, 1991
*Al came home without telling his parents, and he's
sleeping here. It's cool. It's going to be sad saying
good-bye to Pat on Friday. I really like him, and I hate
to see him leave. I got into the University of Arizona
today. I went to Stamford with Kelly and Josh, but we
didn't drink.*

January 20, 1991
*Kate just called me; she wants to get some coke
tomorrow. That's cool. I'll do it. Mark, Al, and I went
to Utopia today, a headshop. Mark and I bought a dug
out. I have a nice bud for it. I feel strange about the
incident at school on Friday. Group with Pat and
Chris was harsh because now I wonder about what
Chris thinks of me. And Dave's meeting with my
mother pisses me off. What right do they have to tell
her that I shouldn't be allowed to go to Arizona? It
was fun having Al sleep over. We got to spend so
much time together. I miss him when he's away at
school. Of course I got high again today, but if anyone
asks on Monday, it's 33 days clean. I think I'm
going to get some coke. I'm glad my parents aren't
sending me to rehab. I knew they wouldn't.*

January 21, 1991
I've already gotten high today. It's 1:50 in the

afternoon and I just woke up. I have no desire to get clean and stay that way. I've been lying about my clean time, but I don't care anymore. I have nothing to hide. I'm an addict and it's gonna take time for me to stop. I can't change my past, but I can improve my future. I don't need a rehab to help me do that.

January 22, 1991
Dave kept asking me what drugs I used over the weekend. I wouldn't talk about it. I don't trust that son of a bitch. I went to Mrs. Brandon's room during second period and confronted her about the meeting with my mother. Kelly, Linda, Barbara, and I were laughing because she didn't have me suspended.

January 23, 1991
Kelly, Josh, Zeke, and Barbara, just left my house. It's 11:30. I have a Physics midterm tomorrow, and I just got baked with them instead of studying. I'm so sad about Pat leaving Friday. I'm not sure what I should say to him. Well, I have zero days clean again. Who cares?

January 24, 1991
I talked to Bob today. I never realized how lucky I am to have him to talk to. He said that he trusts me because he knows me well enough to know when I'm getting too dangerous. I feel like my life is a TV show, and each day I tune in to a new episode. I wonder if I'll cry Friday when I say good-bye to Pat. He was so cool with me. I honestly thought about everything he said to me. I'll miss him. Before him I never got a chance to talk to an adult who actually understands

about drugs. I don't know what to tell him or the people in group what I think about them. Knowing that I have group on Friday is what keeps me going.

January 25, 1991
Pat left today. He gave us a poem, and a couple people read it out loud. Everyone was so sad. I almost cried, but I held it until I was alone in my car. I stopped myself. It was sad. We all gave Pat a hug, and that was it. But he said we could call him if we needed to talk to him. Mr. Kosh has his number. I just got home from volunteering at the hospital. I'm so tired. Today I went to school, to work, and to the hospital. But it feels good to do it. Tomorrow I'm supposed to go to a concert with Krisha. Either way I want to get high. I need to stop using.

    I don't know what to do anymore.

January 26, 1991
I really crave coke bad. I tried to smoke a joint to satisfy my urge to use, but it didn't work. I wish I had a real lot of money so I could buy all the coke I wanted. I'd say, to hell with NA and recovery. Which Chris do I like better? The responsible aspiring physician? Or the drug addict? I went to half an NA meeting and came home. I'm still in a screwed-up mood.

January 27, 1991
I think it was meant for me to become an addict, get kicked out of Lauralton, etc. If I had stayed there I wouldn't have made the new friends I have. My drug use probably would've progressed much worse than it

has. I needed those things to happen. I have no regrets about anything anymore. There isn't reason for me to. My life is going well, and I don't care if anyone says any different. I love my parents and my family. I am very fortunate. Not everyone has the opportunities I've had. I'm doing great. I'm going to college. I want to be a doctor. There's no reason for me to be unhappy. Thank God I never committed suicide or overdosed. That would've been a waste of a promising life. I want to get coke real bad. I'm seriously considering it for tomorrow.

January 28, 1991
I want to change. I need help. I can't do it alone. I've got to stop doing drugs. But I can't do it. I'm so powerless. My life is good, but if it wasn't for the people around me, I don't know what would've happened. I'm very grateful. I'm not afraid to admit my problem. But I'm afraid of abstinence. My life is so complicated. I could easily write a book about it. I want to be successful so bad, and yet I'm plagued by this disease. I don't want to be like this anymore.

January 29, 1991
So many messed-up things have happened in my life. But I wouldn't trade it for anything. I'm a better person for it. Everything is a learning experience. I haven't gotten high at all today. I think I'll go to Brooks and get pipe cleaners so I can clean the dug out. Last night when Mark and I were smoking from it, it clogged, but I kept inhaling anyway and it really wiped my lungs out.

    Drug Free Milford was cool tonight. Mark and I

got baked before going. The speaker was a judge. It was making me nervous. I was shaking. Every time he said the word cocaine and started talking about it my mouth watered. I'm craving bad. Mark and I smoked another bone after the meeting. Today I told Dave I want to change and he said, "Don't tell me that; tell yourself."

January 30, 1991
I've got to get out of my denial. I saw Greg today and he said the usual: "You have a drug problem, and rehab wouldn't be that bad." He says the way I comprehend my situation and talk honestly with him is really cool. But I have a hard time swallowing the things he tells me. He thinks I am very out of control. I think I do have control over my use, at least to some extent. He says I have no chance of staying clean without a change in my environment—inpatient treatment. I'm psyched that I passed all my midterm exams. That's a start. I'm afraid of what's happening to me and my life. It scares the shit out of me when everyone tells me what a big problem I have. It's comforting to know that my parents won't force me to go to rehab. God, I want to do coke so bad. The love I have of cocaine is similar to that which a person feels in a relationship. I have a relationship with the drug. Unfortunately it's one that causes my life to become unmanageable. There is a great deal of insanity that comes along with this addiction. Cocaine is to me what food is to some people. At times, I feel as though I need it to survive. While using it, I tend to want it more intensely after each line, or hit, or injection....It is an insatiable craving. No one but another cocaine

user can understand this feeling.

Tomorrow I'm going to get higher than I ever have before. I have to. It's a need; I need that shit as much as I need to breathe. Just thinking about it makes me feel better.

I did do cocaine on January 31. It was the last time I used the drug. It was also the closest I have ever come to death. Over the course of a few hours I inhaled six grams. It was sick. I overdosed and used again. I did that a few times. I had a whiteout. I coughed up white foam. My heart froze for what seemed like an hour. It was a terrifying experience. But I wanted more, I couldn't get enough. It was suicidal. I'm not sure what I was trying to prove. Originally I had wanted to shoot it, but I decided to just snort it instead. I did line after line. I knew that there was something wrong with the whole situation. I finally realized that I couldn't do cocaine anymore. I was going to die if I kept it up.

That happened on my first day of substance abuse class with Dave Ullman. It was a Thursday, the day before my first group with Chris running it. I got home that night still high, and while suffering through my shaking and cold sweats at two o'clock in the morning, I asked myself if I really needed to go to rehab. I knew what the answer was, and going to inpatient treatment began to enter my mind as a possibility.

February 1, 1991
We had our first group with Chris Burke today. I like him. He's cool. Of course, practically the first words out of his mouth were, "You should go to inpatient." I asked the group, "How many people think I should go to rehab?" They all raised their hands. Then as usual, Ullman had to tell me when I saw him that he thinks I

should go, too. He said he feels bad for me because my life is a mess. I was whining about how unfair it is that this is happening to me. I have no one to blame but myself. In a way I'd like to throw in the towel and go to rehab, but I like to solve my own problems. Pete said it's like going to camp. Well, the issue is moot because my parents would never let me go even if I wanted to. They'd deny that I have a problem. I can't believe I did this to my life.

I cannot wait to go to school in the fall. It's going to be great. Even if I do manage to get clean, I'll still party at ASU. Pete and Kelly both went to rehab and they still drink. So maybe I'll just drink and smoke pot. That wouldn't be so bad.

Before the school year started I made a goal for myself that I would not be using anymore by the end of the year. As long as I start showing some improvement, I think that everyone will back off about the rehab issue. I don't want to use anything this weekend, kind of as a test for myself. I really want to be able to go to school on Monday feeling good both physically and mentally and honestly say that I have three days clean. I think I can do it.

February 2, 1991
I worked at the hospital tonight. I had a long conversation with a lady whose sister was in on a heroin overdose. I talked to her about coke because she said, "You look like you do cocaine, right?" It was strange that she could tell. I almost asked her if she wanted to leave right then and go pick up some coke. Especially after she told me about her old freebasing habit.

February 3, 1991
I just woke up, and the first thing that entered my mind was, Am I going to stay clean today? I hope so. What would life be like drug free? I'm afraid to find out. I think I'm functioning well. Greg said I still function, but not nearly as well as I could. He said I have no control over my life or my drug use. I've known for a while now that I have little or no control, and I know that should scare me, but it doesn't. I carried weed with me last night. I knew I wasn't going to use. I was afraid of going out and not being able to get high if I wanted to. I don't need to go to rehab; I can handle myself and my use. No, that's not true.

I've got to stop kidding myself. I am an addict, and I can't change that. It sucks, but it's my reality. I need help. It's so strange to have all these people involved in my life, when last year I was suffering by myself. Why did this have to happen to me? My life was not supposed to turn out like this.

I just went out to the kitchen and I saw the vodka bottle. I wanted to grab it and just drink it right from the bottle. I'm out of control. I want to get baked tomorrow. No one has to know. I could get high every day and not tell anyone. It's my own fault that I hear this rehab shit every day.

February 4, 1991
I went to the nurse's office today to get some water and because I felt real dizzy. She called Dave down from his class to talk to me. I wanted to tell him that I've been considering rehab. I guess I kind of got that through to him. I have the feeling of just wanting to get high and say screw everything. I wish I could

wake up one morning and have all this behind me. What if I tell my parents that I want to go to rehab and they decide I'm too unstable to go to Arizona? I need to go to school there. I have my heart set on it. I can't even imagine saying to my parents, "I have a cocaine problem and I need help." I could never do it. What would my grandparents say? They'd think I was a scumbag. If someone told me last year that this would be happening to me, I would have laughed. I never thought this would happen to me. I don't know why I'm having such a hard time kicking this. I think about using, and that's it. I just lose it.

I went to an NA meeting tonight and I was the second person to share, and I did for about ten minutes. I just let it all go—the rehab shit, my love of cocaine, everything. The people there all told me I should go to treatment. It really makes me think.

February 5, 1991
I got ripped this afternoon at the restaurant where Mark works. His boss was away and Mark had to do some work so we stayed there for about three hours and I drank beer from the keg. I had five shots of vodka before I picked him up to go.

I smoked some weed, too. I was miserable, though. I just sat there and thought about whether or not I should go to rehab. I brought my NA Recovery Text. It was the worst time I ever had drinking, and I drank alone, too. It was depressing. It isn't fun anymore.

I just got up to answer the phone, and I thought I was going to have a heart attack. I'm having severe chest pains. Just what I need. I went jogging with

Kelly tonight, after I got drunk. It was fun. I'm surprised that I didn't get sick.

I can't wait to go to Arizona to start my life over. I don't need to go to rehab, I need to start living life on life's terms. And if that means stopping all of my use—both drugs and alcohol—then that's what I'll do. There is no need for me to tell my mother that I have a cocaine problem she doesn't need the stress. I'm going to do my best to abstain from all drugs. Maybe this week was my bottom, the whole month of January even. Maybe it took me almost going to treatment to let me see how messed up I am. But I can handle it. I've got a new perspective on myself.

February 6, 1991
I met with Greg this morning. He has an appointment with my mother tomorrow morning and he's decided that he's going to tell her that I have a drug problem and inpatient treatment is the only thing that can save me.

In a way, I'm relieved. There's a way to go through with this now. He said not to worry because no matter what my parents say or do, I won't be alone. I know that's true. I have a lot of friends, and it's a good feeling to know that. Without their support, I'm nothing. The whole decision rests upon what I say to my mother when I get home from work tomorrow night. I can either admit that I have a problem and need help, or I can minimize and deny it all. I shared at a meeting tonight, and I've decided to accept the rehab plan.

My Spanish teacher asked me today what is wrong with me, why I miss class so often. She asked me if I have a problem with drugs and alcohol. I didn't get into it with her.

Pete was telling me about his rehab and how he enjoyed it. He had himself admitted. I'll never get anywhere if I don't start accepting responsibility for myself. It may turn out to be the best thing for me. Everyone is trying to help me, and I'd be stupid not to accept it. I can't go to Arizona in August in the state of mind I'm in now. I don't want to die, I want to enjoy the rest of my life. I'm only 17. That's way too young to die.

February 7, 1991
Well, I'm going to inpatient. But my parents found out about it from me and not Greg. He canceled his appointment with my mother today and I think it worked out for the best that I told them. My parents took it well. I just came right out and told my mother that I'm addicted to cocaine, and I'm going to die if I don't go to rehab. It was the hardest thing I've ever had to say to them. They understand how I feel because they've been there, too. I'm glad that they're being so supportive. Mark is sad that I'm going. I wish my friends could visit me. I want to go to Wakeman Hall. I'm not going to Arms Acres in New York, that's for sure. If I go to Wakeman I'll be able to see Chris Burke, and it's closer to home, too. My mother is meeting with Greg tomorrow morning. He should be pleased that I told her. Chris Burke ought to be happy to hear my decision, too. I think it's really going to work out for me. I feel a lot of pressure has been lifted already. I want to go for 30 days, not 45. It seems like such a long time.

Greg Ryan tried to get me into Wakeman Hall, but he didn't call the right office. He called a cottage at the Children's Center, where Wakeman is located, and they said that they couldn't accept a new admission. Not realizing that he wasn't speaking to someone at Wakeman, he thought Wakeman was full and set me up at Arms Acres.

February 8, 1991
I'm leaving for Arms Acres in New York tomorrow. In group, Chris was concerned with my wanting to wait a few days before I left. He wanted to bring me to Wakeman himself. But I have to go to Arms Acres now. I can't bring this journal or anything else. I'm ready I guess. Al, Mark, Jill, Ralph, and Dee came over tonight. I talked to Mrs. Holm and Amy on the phone. I told Mike, Krisha, and Rachel what was going on. I smoked pot for my last time with Grant and Dan after school in my car, with the dug out. I thought I would be leaving next week when I did it. I didn't get a chance to say good-bye to anyone at school. I wrote Sandy in California a letter tonight, because I'll be in rehab during her birthday. I'll be gone for 35 days, and I'll be home March 16. My mother is handling it extremely well. The only books I can bring are the Bible and my NA text. I can bring six packs of cigarettes, blank notebooks, and there's no music and no hair dryer. It's a possibility that they'll take me off Elavil. Dave told me he has never seen me look as alive and well as I did today. I had a good day in school. The whole thing really hasn't hit me yet. It will tomorrow when we're driving up there. I can't wait to get it over with.

Grant and Dan were the last two friends I used with. Grant was also the last person I sold pot to. I sold him the first bag of weed he ever paid for. We often sat in Physics and read the magazine *High Times*. Although we used to talk about drugs a lot, when I finally started trying to stay sober he was one of the most supportive of my friends. He still is. Sometimes I bother him about his own use, but I try not to. I can only worry about staying clean myself.

CHAPTER NINE

My mother and I took our time getting to Arms Acres. It was a Saturday. We stopped at a mall to eat my last lunch on the outside. I smoked all the cigarettes I could. As we pulled into the driveway at Arms Acres, I was having second thoughts about going in. There was a knot in my stomach as I realized that I was giving up my freedom for 35 days. My heart was pounding as I got out of the car. I felt like I was walking down death row. It was a nice building, and I thought it looked like a cool place. It was big, although I'd never seen another treatment center to compare it to. Inside it was clean and modern with the atmosphere of a hospital. We waited in a little room in admitting. When it was our turn, we answered questions together and separately and signed about a million forms. A man from AA came in and asked where I was from. He told me he'd find people in the program for me to get in touch with upon my release. I was trying my best to be calm, but I felt sick when the head adolescent counselor came in and took me into a little examining room to change into my greens, a surgeon's outfit of green shirt and pants. It was my last moment with my clothes. A nurse came in and searched me. She really didn't watch me as I undressed. I just had to show her that I wasn't hiding anything in my socks and underwear.

For the next two hours I filled out questionnaires while my mother waited down the hall. Finally, three hours after we'd arrived, they had me say good-bye to my mother. I felt choked up, like I was going to cry, but I held back, mostly for her sake. I knew it must've been hard enough to leave her child at a rehab. I didn't want her to leave with me all upset. They gave her the items that I couldn't have: my hair conditioner, lotion, the clothes I'd arrived in, my shoes, razors, cough drops, candy, gum, NA text, notebook. Pretty much everything I brought I couldn't have. We hugged and said good-bye. That was it. As soon as I went back to detox, I started crying. I couldn't stop. All the adults there were wondering what was wrong with me, and I thought I'd never stop.

While I was crying, a nurse who had already been annoying me came over and asked me what was wrong. She called me "little girl." I snapped. I started screaming at her, "What do you think's wrong, bitch?" After that she walked away. I sat there for about half an hour, and they brought me a dinner tray. It was like being in the hospital. I heard the annoying nurse talking on the phone with the psychiatrist on call. She was telling him that I had a suicide history and I had gone off on her and maybe I'd be better off in a psychiatric hospital. I jumped up and started walking down the hall. She got off the phone and came after me. I said I was going to call my parents because there was no way I was going to stay in that place. I said, "Give me a phone." She and another nurse started explaining how I wasn't allowed to use the phone. I grabbed the phone from the desk and threw it at the wall. They sent me into the adult lounge to calm down. Some guy gave me a cigarette, but the nurse saw and wouldn't let me smoke it. When the adolescent counselors came to bring me to the unit, I told them I wanted a phone. Of course they said no, and I just went with them. I figured that it was my own fault I was there so I might as well stick it out.

I finally went on the unit and I met the other kids in Phase One. My roommate, Erin, and Brett, Sam, and Jack. It was time for smoke break and it was such a relief to smoke. The counselors left the room and I got to know the other kids a little. I kept saying over and over how I couldn't believe I was there. Bill, a counselor, came in and told us it was time for recreation. He had us go into the hall because we were going to play the "fruit" game. It's hard to explain the game, but it was fun and I started to feel a little better about the place. After that we had a lecture and saw a movie about drugs and alcohol. My roommate told me that she was going to a halfway house in New York the next night. We talked for a while about what it was like to be at Arms Acres.

We were in a two-person room. It was larger than I'd expected. There was plenty of room for two people to stay out of each other's way. There were two beds, two dressers, and a desk with two chairs. The carpet was a drab green, with curtains to match. There was a lamp on each dresser and one on the desk, so there was plenty of lighting. Each room had a bathroom and a large closet. It was similar to an ugly hotel room. The bathroom door locked, but the entrance door to the room had no lock on it. The bathroom had a sink, toilet, shower, and medicine cabinet. It was designed to be used by one person at a time. We had 15 minutes each to use the bathroom in the morning. Each day a maid came in to clean the bathroom and make sure we had enough towels, toilet paper, soap, etc. Our room wasn't very homey, though. It had a cold, hospital kind of feeling. We controlled the temperature ourselves, but it was always either too hot or too cold. The window was the sliding type, but it was bolted to open only three inches. There was no clock. It seemed very bare. But it was roomy and clean, and I was happy to have a bathroom.

I didn't sleep very well my first night. I was tense. I ended up talking to Erin about why we were there and how the place operated until we fell asleep.

The next day, Sunday, we were allowed to sleep until 7:00 instead of 6:00. A girl from Phase Two had to wake us up. She brought us our greens. Erin took her shower and then woke me up. The first thing that we did after showering was have a smoke break. We all gathered in the break room for 15 minutes. Then we made our beds and cleaned up our rooms. After that we had breakfast, which was in the Phase Two kitchen because Phase One couldn't eat in the dining room. The food was terrible, which didn't bother me much because I had no appetite. Since we ate on the unit, the quality of the food was lower than in the dining room. Food was delivered to the unit in a metal cabinet about six feet high, in stainless steel bins covered with plastic wrap. It was not at all appetizing. The only beverage was milk and, occasionally, juice. I'd eaten better meals on airplanes. After breakfast we had easy chores to do, like vacuuming the hallway and cleaning the windows in the break room. On Sunday we had meditation in the community room downstairs. All adult and adolescent patients were brought in. A lady had everyone sing two "inspirational" songs. I had no interest in singing. It was like church. I think the lady was some kind of pastor.

Then we went back onto the unit for group. It was my first group therapy session there, and I had to introduce myself. I told the other kids why I was there. The session lasted an hour and a half, with a smoke break before lunch. Once again the food sucked. We had an AA meeting in the afternoon. Every minute of the day we had some kind of activity related to recovery and substance-abuse education. We even talked about it during meals. The only time we didn't talk about it was recreation. It was intense. I was trying to have a good attitude, but it was hard. We couldn't do anything. Not only was there no music, we couldn't whistle, sing, or hum.

There were so many rules. If we were in an AA meeting, girls and boys couldn't sit on the same couch. If it wasn't time for bed or after 10:00 P.M., we couldn't touch our beds. Not at all. Not even during quiet time weekdays, between 5:00 and 5:30 P.M. We always had to sit on chairs at our desks when in our rooms. In the morning we had meditation in the unit, where we would read out of a meditation book and state a goal for the day. We had group twice a day, a total of three hours.

Within the first 24 hours at Arms Acres, I was told who would be my case manager. The case manager was one of the adolescent counselors. Mine was Judith. She was the one I would go to with any problems I had or if I needed to have her call my parents to have them bring me something on Saturdays, when they had to attend the family program.

Erin left for her halfway house late Sunday night and was gone when I woke up on Monday. I was now the only girl on Phase One. There were two girls on Phase Two but I wasn't allowed to talk to them. Phase One can last up to 14 days. You can't talk to your parents or see them while on Phase One. You can only correspond by mail. You have to complete several projects to get to Phase Two. When you get there, you get your clothes back. There were about 20 kids on Phase Two when I was in Phase One.

Before Erin left she managed to cause some trouble. A girl in Phase Two snuck her a cigarette and Erin hid it in our room. Eventually she told all of us. But Brett, who was trying hard to abide by all the rules, found out and ratted on her. The staff tore apart our room looking for it. It was a big thing to the staff, although I didn't consider it all that serious. They finally found it, and we all lost a smoke break. They interrogated all of us and wanted to know why none of us had ratted on her. Everyone was pissed at Brett because Erin was going to share the cigarette. The staff said I was responsible for her because we were roommates. It was a great way to start my stay there.

I had "intervention" on Monday. The parents and significant others were to come in with a list of statements that wrapped up how the user had hurt the family members. I was pulled out of afternoon group for mine. I was led into a room where my mother sat. We weren't allowed to talk to each other at all, but we said hi. The intervention lasted about 45 seconds, or so it seemed. My mother read four statements to me, mostly about how she and my father were hurt that I'd kept my problem from them for so long. Then I had to get up and leave. It was so hard. I went back to group and started crying. We spent the rest of group talking about what my mother had said and how I felt about it. I thought intervention was a pretty shitty thing to do. In group that time they also gave me an affirmation that I had to say every time I introduced myself in group. I had to say, "I'm Chris. I'm an addict and an alcoholic, don't let me hide my true feelings. What I don't say will kill me."

When I finally got a chance, I tried to write a journal entry in the notebook Arms Acres provided for me:

Monday night, February 11, 1991
I think that I made the right decision coming into
treatment. It's hard to get adjusted to, but in the long

run it might save my life. My denial is what led to the rapid progression of my disease toward the end. The substitution of one drug for another was a big obstacle for me to overcome. I thought that it would be okay if I smoked pot or drank, because at least I wasn't using cocaine. Now I realize that a drug is a drug is a drug. I abuse any drug I come into contact with. There is no safe way for me to use. The next time I use cocaine I might die, but my disease tells me that I won't die, that I can control my use. But I can't. Abstaining from cocaine while using other drugs always led me back to the coke. I would have done anything for that drug. And knowing that I feel that way scares the shit out of me. I didn't ask to become a drug addict or alcoholic, but I am, and I will remain so for the rest of my life. My recovery is the greatest gift I have ever received. I just plan to work my program to the best of my ability and live just for today.

I had the room to myself that night. I made a promise to myself to pray at least once every day. That night I got on my knees and prayed for God to give me a sign that he really exists. I asked for strength. It felt good. I needed to fill the void that I felt when I made the conscious decision to give up drugs and alcohol.

By the end of Monday I had already completed two assignments that had to be accomplished to move into Phase Two. They were a chemical dependency symptoms checklist and a psychological history. I wanted to get everything I could out of treatment. I forced myself to be positive.

I wrote letters constantly, to both friends and family. My first night I think I wrote about four letters.

After quiet time, before dinner, we had a little group

called Community Commitments. There we said what we would contribute individually to the community. If we were at a loss for what our commitment would be, we would just offer our support. At night, right before we went to our rooms, we had "highs and lows." We read a page of a meditation book and told about the high and the low of our day. We rated our day on a scale of one to ten. There were always structured activities such as the groups, lectures, fitness, meetings—never any free time. We could look at a schedule on the wall and follow it exactly. It was all planned out.

Tuesday I got a new roommate. Her name was Jessica. She was 15 years old. The first time she smoked crack was at age 8. We got along very well. It was her second time in Arms Acres. She was on a New York PINS (Persons in Need of Support) Petition, which meant she was a ward of the state. She had been in rehabs for the past year. She looked old. Her appearance was that of a beaten person. By that I mean that she had already lived a life of hell for a person her age. She really had a lot to offer me, and I realized that. Our counselors warned me to look at her and see that it was like looking in a mirror because although she was younger than me, I would be just like her if I kept using. That scared me.

Tuesday and Wednesday mornings I was awakened at five o'clock for blood testing. Tuesday I was still waking up shaking with cold sweats. I took a shower and was led down for blood drawing. After they drew my blood I sat at a desk in detox and almost passed out. I couldn't see. Everything was in black and white. I whispered to a nurse and she ran over and took my blood pressure. It was 60/30. She didn't believe it, so she did it twice more with the same results. About 20 minutes later I didn't feel much better, and the orange juice they were making me drink was making me sick. About an hour later my blood pressure went up to 94/57. They gave me a cigarette. I ate breakfast with the adults in detox, and they gave me cigarettes, too, so I was happy. Two hours later I returned to the unit.

We got another kid on Phase One, Tom. I really got a kick out of him. He epitomized the stereotypical "burnout." He let his hair hang in his face and walked with a slight slouch. His voice was slow and mellow, and he often threw in words like *man* and *yo*. He tried to act dumb, but he wasn't. He liked giving people an attitude. We all got along well. My roommate, Jessica, and I talked quite a bit. We were the only coke addicts on Phase One. Everyone else was mainly involved with alcohol and pot. Jessica and I were thought of by them as "worse" because we had lowered ourselves to drinking things like vanilla extract and NyQuil. The others had never tried coke, except Tom. He, Jessica, and I often talked. It wasn't unusual for Jessica and me to stay up half the night talking.

I got a card from my grandparents on Valentine's Day. It was a surprise to me because I hadn't told them I was going away. I hadn't wanted to hurt them. I was thrilled to have mail, though. The next day I got a card from my parents.

By Thursday I was really getting frustrated with Arms Acres and its stupid rules. I started feeling a need to go home and start working things out on my own. I began to lose my positive attitude. Finally on Friday, during fitness, I almost caused a brawl between Sam and Tom. We were playing floor hockey, and I wasn't in the mood for it. I was standing around and walking, but I refused to participate actively. Soon Tom was copying my poor attitude. Sam said something to him about trying to get the rest of them in trouble. They almost got into a fistfight and Tom ended up kicking a hole in the gymnasium wall.

I finished my chemical history that morning. It wasn't entirely accurate, of course, but I thought that I was able to detail it quite well. I was going to present it in group that afternoon. After fitness, however, I made the decision that I was going to leave. During the half-hour break before group, Jessica told me I could leave if I gave 72 hours notice. I decided to do it. I wrote the necessary letter, giving notice and promising to stay clean and sober at home, attend daily NA or AA meetings, call my sponsor at least daily, go to weekly sessions with my substance abuse counselor, and submit to regular drug testing.

Link, a counselor, and Kris, the manager, were shocked when I handed them my notice. I did it calmly and walked back into the break room. The entire group was focused on Tom and me handing in our notices. Everyone defended me. I was really hostile to Link and Judith.

After group, Kris called my mother to tell her that I'd given my notice. She was hesitant about letting me come home, which is understandable after hearing what I'd been doing. I was allowed to talk to her, but not privately, and that kept me from saying why I really wanted to come home. I wanted to leave because I felt like I needed to be with my parents and work things out. I wanted to go to my own meetings and start working on my recovery.

After I hung up I went on with the usual day. It was time to have dinner and I had to get an EKG. After that I went back up to the unit. At about seven-thirty Judith called me in to talk to my mother on the phone again. Judith took the phone from me after a couple minutes and told my mother that I was manipulating her and maybe she should let me leave but not come home. I started yelling at her. I got the phone back and I talked to my father. He said that if I really wanted to come home I could. They would take me home the next day after the family program. I walked out of the room after Judith hung up. The kids on Phase One were laughing. They'd heard me screaming.

Judith called me into her office and Link came in. They told me I was going to die if I left. I went off on them and when I really started getting pissed I picked up a chair and threw it. Link was yelling at me, and I just walked out.

Jessica was the only incentive for me to reconsider leaving; she and I were having fun in our own way. But her stay at Arms Acres wasn't secure enough for me to base my decision on. She could leave any day to go to a therapeutic community. She was really an interesting person. She snorted water one night on my dresser in our room. She said it cleared her sinuses. I tried it but didn't find it that helpful. The next night, she made herself pass out on the floor in our room. She was very interesting.

At 8:30, we had our AA meeting. Phase One and Phase Two attended the AA meetings together. During the smoke break before it we got a new admission, Bill. He was pretty young and very depressed, not unusual for someone going into rehab. We were all discussing what was going on with Tom and me. Tom's parents had come in to see him about giving his notice, because they didn't live very far away. They told him they weren't going to give him permission to leave even though he had admitted himself. At the AA meeting no one shared long enough to fill up the meeting time. It was the quietest meeting since I had been there. After everyone had shared, Cindie, the chair, asked if anyone wanted to share again. No one else raised their hands, so I did. I said that I was leaving the next day and I was sorry that I hadn't gotten to know the kids in Phase Two better. I wished everyone luck. After me, a couple kids shared about how I should stay and how they wanted to get to know me better, too. Then Tom raised his hand and said he was sorry that I was leaving but he was glad I was getting out before the staff could mess my head up. A staff member took him out of the room after that.

That night several counselors came in to try to convince me to stay. I was pretty rude to them because they were pissing me off. When they realized that I wasn't going to change my mind easily, they all told me that I was going to die and they gave me a month to live at the most. A doctor came up and said that my EKG showed palpitations. If I continued to use coke I would die. I told them all to go to hell, I was going to stay clean.

My roommate and I had a long talk. She said that she thought I was going to make it, and if I ever went to use again, I should just think of her and of how I didn't want to end up like that. It really meant a lot to me. She was right. I didn't want to be like she was. She was one of the most incredible people I have ever met. She was sincere. I hope that she's doing well. She has a lot to offer.

The day I was leaving Arms Acres people did their best to get me to stay. After the AA meeting the night before, Cindie, Sarah, and Jon, three kids from Phase Two, had asked if they could talk to me the next morning about staying. So we went into a little office on the unit, just the four of us without any staff. They related their own experiences and why they had come to Arms Acres. Jon and Sarah both said cocaine was their favorite drug. Cindie was an alcoholic. It was touching, because they really cared about me and my sobriety. For a minute I almost considered staying. I would have been Sarah's roommate on Phase Two. They shared a lot of personal things with me. Very personal. Sarah had had an abortion while at Arms Acres. She shared about how drugs had almost ruined her life. They had been informed of my chemical history, and Sarah and Jon were saying how much they had related to me in meetings.

Then Link came in. He ruined the nice atmosphere we had. He asked how we had been doing, and I said, "Fine until you came in." We all talked for a while and then Jon, Cindie, and Sarah left the room. They all wished me luck. Link and I talked for a while and I explained to him why I thought I could make it when I left. I told him I was seriously considering going to Wakeman Hall, a rehab near Milford, when I got home. I wasn't really, but it was an option. Once again Link told me that I was going to die, and he didn't think I had any chance of making it with my chemical history.

Before lunch, Jessica and I had to get our daily medicine at the nurse's desk in detox. My parents were sitting next to the hall that we walked through. I said to Jessica, "Hey, that's my parents."

The counselor who was with us said, "Don't talk to them." So I said "Hi" and she gave me a dirty look. She was only the art therapist so I didn't take her too seriously. After we got our meds and were walking back, my parents were still sitting there. I said, "I'm ready whenever you are."

My mother goes, "You have a BFA," which meant "bad fucking attitude."

Since it was a Saturday, we didn't have much to do. Group was very tense. But when Link and Judith tried to start with me, everybody defended me, saying that they knew I was going to make it. I was very defensive and hostile toward the staff. After lunch we watched a movie, *Lord of the Flies*, for recreation. I was very impatient because I had to wait to leave. I was dying to change into my clothes again. It felt like the movie was dragging on forever. It was almost over when they called me out to see my parents. I was led into the same room where I had the meeting with Jon, Sarah, and Cindie that morning. I was with my parents, Judith, and Kristen, a family therapist. I had to read my chemical history out loud. That was really hard and I could tell my parents were a bit surprised at what they heard. The grand totals of my use were approximately 51,108 ounces of alcohol, about 4,344 joints worth of marijuana, 1,083 grams of cocaine, 1,770 pills of speed, and 9 hits of LSD. Judith tried to use my totals as a way to manipulate my parents into making me stay. I got really hostile toward Kristen and Judith. When they finally realized that I wasn't going to stay, they gave my parents their last chance to make me stay, and that was it. They told me I was going "against medical advice."

I called Mark the minute I got home. He was surprised to hear from me. It was great to talk to him. I went to an NA meeting right away with my friend Kris, who was in group with me at Foran. It was a step meeting, and there happened to be a speaker that night. It was really interesting. It was also an anniversary meeting, celebrating one year for the meeting. I knew many of the people there, and it felt good to be with them. That night I enjoyed my freedom more than I ever had. I felt like I had been released from prison. The only thing was, I knew that everyone like Greg, Dave, and Chris Burke were all going to be on my back about finishing treatment. I expected it. I knew that things weren't over yet. I made a commitment to stay clean, though.

The next night I went to a meeting in New Haven that I'd never been to. I got my first NA key chain. It said Just For Today on it. I was sure that I could quit using on an outpatient basis. I knew that I was going to enjoy sobriety. Not everyone was as sure as I was that I could stay clean. Dave told me one day that he didn't think I could do it on my own. He said, "It isn't you I don't trust. It's your addiction."

I got rid of all my drug paraphernalia. The last thing I got rid of was my dug out, which I gave to a friend at school. It had been in the glove compartment of the car that I'd bought shortly after totaling the first one. By the end of February I believed that recovery really was making me a better person. When I was using, I had never realized how much I was hurting.

Then I decided that it might be a good idea for me to go to Wakeman Hall in Hamden for outpatient treatment. I called Chris Burke and told him my idea. Then I met him at Wakeman to look at the place and hear about the different programs they offered. It was a really cool-looking place compared to Arms Acres. Although Arms Acres was a newer and more modern facility, Wakeman was much more homey. The atmosphere seemed very relaxed. I didn't go up to see the unit that day, but from what I did see, I thought it wouldn't be a bad idea to go there. I heard about the different programs and was told that, theoretically, I could go to inpatient for 14 days, which didn't seem bad at all to me. I said I would think about it.

Everyone was telling me how much I had changed from before. I felt different, but I didn't think the change was that drastic. I did feel a need to make amends to everyone whom I'd hurt. I started with Lauralton and made my amends to Mrs. Gates and Mrs. Johnson. I told them I was sorry for everything I had done there, and that I was an addict and an alcoholic. It felt great. They were really overwhelmed, I think. They told me that I was a courageous and strong person to be able to go back and say that to them. Seeing Greg that morning had made me decide to do it. He also helped me decide to go to Wakeman for two weeks.

The next day I announced my decision in group at Foran, and a Milford *Citizen* reporter was there. The reporter was sitting in on group, and when I started talking she became very interested in my story. She asked a few questions about Lauralton and my drug history. She wrote down a lot of things about me, and I didn't think anything of it because I had just told the truth. That day after school I went back up to Wakeman and Chris showed me the rest of the place. I set it up to go in on Monday.

Over the weekend I volunteered in the emergency room, and Mark came with me. I also talked to Al. It was strange not feeling like, Oh, I want to get drunk. Things really seemed to have changed. Sunday I went to my grandfather's birthday party and enjoyed my last day of freedom for two weeks. In my journal I wrote, "I wish I had never gotten involved with drugs and alcohol. This is something I never thought would happen to me. Everything is so different now; my relationships with my family and friends have changed drastically. In a way, I feel relieved."

My mother and I got to Wakeman at 2:00 on Monday, and we ended up waiting awhile before seeing anyone from admissions because there was another girl coming in at the same time. After we sat down with the woman from admissions, we spent about 45 minutes getting all the paperwork and details set. Since I was still taking Elavil, we found out that we had to go to the VA hospital to get a note from my neurologist authorizing my prescription. I didn't mind that at all, because it meant that we got to go out in public again. It bought me some extra freedom.

I smoked as many cigarettes as possible. At the VA hospital I walked by a conference room and saw Bob Novelly in a meeting. It calmed me down a bit to see him. He's the coolest psychologist I've ever met. When we finally saw the lady who was giving us the note, my mother got into a conversation about why I needed it. She told the lady I was on my way to rehab and everything. I didn't mind. It was good for her to be talking about it. After we left the hospital and went back to Wakeman, it didn't take long before I got admitted. I said good-bye to my mother and they took me up to the unit.

When I got up to the unit at Wakeman I was much more relaxed than I had been at Arms Acres. The stereo was on in the dayroom and that was a good sign. The kids were all really friendly and so was the staff. I think that getting to wear our own clothes and keep personal things like books made a big difference. There were pictures on the walls and it wasn't a hospital atmosphere at all. Another new admission, Julie, had come upstairs about five minutes before me. We were all on the unit, where most of our waking time was spent. There was a dayroom, a conference room, a few offices, a kitchen, and a laundry room. When I arrived, we were about to have dinner in the dayroom, which was unusual. Weekday meals were usually eaten in the dining room.

Right before dinner everyone did introductions. This allowed us to get to know more about people than just their names. For example, to every new admission I would say, "Hi, I'm Chris, I'm 18 and from Milford. I've been here __ days. My drugs of choice were cocaine, alcohol, and pot."

After dinner we had a cigarette break. Then it was time for chores. Since I'd just arrived, I had to give a urine sample and get searched. That night we had an AA meeting and I felt pretty comfortable at it.

In the morning, Julie and I had to wake up first because we were the newest. There were two showers, so two people could be in the bathroom at the same time. I put all of my stuff in my room. (Everything had been searched during the night.) The only things I couldn't have were my stamps and the saline spray I was using at the time to prevent nosebleeds caused by all my cocaine use.

If we didn't have any chores to do we could just hang out in our rooms. After everyone was showered, we went down for breakfast. Then there were more chores. My chore was cleaning the kitchen, which was on the day unit. It was easy during the week, because all meals were eaten in the dining room. After all the chores were done, we had a cigarette break and then a meeting in the conference room. We stated a goal for the day and said how we were doing.

School started at 8:30 and ended at 12:30. It was the most boring four hours of the day by far. I tried to do all the work in my classes according to where I had left off at Foran. But the teachers were no help at teaching me what I needed to learn. Julie and I both had that problem.

Lunch was at 12:45. We had a smoke first. I didn't like the way Wakeman did smoke breaks at all. We went for hours without a cigarette. After lunch, we had group.

Groups at Wakeman were different from those at Arms Acres mostly because they didn't focus solely on drugs and alcohol. We could discuss anything that we thought was pressing. The staff encouraged us to discuss our family issues, friends, and any other aspect of life.

Every day group had a different theme. One day we had separate men's and women's groups. The girls went into one room and the guys went into a different room. We wrote down questions that we'd always wanted to ask the other group. I can't remember anything specific except that the guys asked pretty sexual questions. Another day we had to ask questions from *The Book of Questions,* and each person in the room had to give an answer.

We also had art therapy, which I never took too seriously. And plain old groups, where we just talked about issues in our lives.

Treatment also consisted of meeting with our therapists. I met with mine, Betsy, twice a week. First we usually talked about how things were going at Wakeman. Then we'd go into what I was going to do to maintain my recovery when I got home. We discussed what we were going to bring up in family therapy that week, and overall what my parents and our relationship were like.

My first whole day we went out to the yard at the Children's Center for recreation time. We just hung out. Julie and I sat around and talked to Ralph, the supervisor. I liked him a lot. He was cool. After that we had rest period. Unlike Arms Acres, it was an hour and a half long. We went to our rooms and did whatever we wanted. We were allowed to sleep if that's what we felt like doing. Mostly I read books and wrote in my journal. Then we had dinner. After dinner we did our chores again. Then we had a community meeting because it was a Tuesday. It was a lot like group therapy. We brought up any issues we had, requested level changes, and made suggestions to better the community. The community consisted of the people in inpatient, and during the day it encompassed all the patients at Wakeman Hall, including partial and aftercare.

When you enter Wakeman, you're automatically on Level 1, which allows you all the basic privileges, such as going to outside meetings, smoking, and weekly phone call. You get a level drop by doing a serious thing, such as going AWOL, refusing a staff member's orders, fighting, anything along those lines. After the first week you can apply for Level 2, which allows more privileges, such as an extra phone call, assigning chores for the community, running community meetings, and listening to a Walkman during free time. Beyond Level 2 there are Levels 3 and 4, which allow even more privileges.

March 5, 1991
Well, I'm here and it's not that bad at all. Only 13 more days left. I should be leaving the 18th. Now that I'm here, though, I don't want to be. I think I could've

stayed sober at home. But the school never would have left me alone. Two weeks is nothing, though.

Last night as I was falling asleep I made a gratitude list in my head. I was up to 140 people and places before I fell asleep.

I'm really glad I didn't stay at Arms Acres. That place makes me appreciate it here a lot. Things will get even better here, I'm sure. I'll definitely give it my best effort. I have 24 days clean.

It's about 4:00 P.M. now. It's been a pretty good day. We went outside for a while. I met my therapist, Betsy. We had a cool conversation. Harold is my primary counselor, like a case manager, I guess. I see my parents Thursday. When I looked in the mirror before, I swear to God I looked different, maybe older. I know that I've changed a lot. I don't need to live that screwed-up life anymore.

March 6, 1991
Chris Burke came today and we got to talk. Now I'm questioning myself and my treatment. I don't think I'm getting anything out of this. I don't feel like I'm addressing the issues that I need to address. I'm all confused. It's like there's emotion in me, but I'm afraid to feel it. The day that Pat left I almost cried, but I went out to my car to be alone to do it. I know that it's an unhealthy thing for me to do. I should just let it out. There are things I really should start talking about. The more I talk here, the easier it's gonna be to get home.

We're going to an outside Cocaine Anonymous meeting tonight. I've only gone to CA once before. I've been thinking about cocaine a lot lately. I'm not craving it or anything, I just think about it.

We had NA, AA, and CA meetings on and off the unit. Only residents went to the meetings on the unit, but one or two addicts or alcoholics from the Area Hospitals and Institutions Committee would chair the meeting. They were usually speaker meetings, so an addict would come in and share his or her story. Then we could also share on what the speaker said or something else we needed to talk about.

The treatment seemed very easy compared to Arms Acres. Instead of the staff hounding us all day to release our feelings in groups, Wakeman encouraged more self-help and reflection. But I wanted the staff to give me a hard time and badger me. I didn't know where to begin on my own.

We could also talk to staff outside of groups and meetings. I liked to talk with Gary, a counselor, about the Twelve Steps, the principles of recovery, and just how to stay clean. Ralph and I talked about the program and our pasts. I talked to Harold, my primary, a lot, too. I liked them because they didn't make me feel like some scumbag kid. I felt like we were friends, the same way I got to feel about people in meetings.

One of the hardest things to get adjusted to at Wakeman was that the staff gave consequences for swearing. It is very difficult for me not to be able to swear at all. Consequences are given for violating rules, and can be anything from writing a paper to being restricted to only speaking to people of your sex.

> *March 7, 1991*
> *I talked to Pat quickly this morning. It was good to see him. He said he was "more than happy" to see me here. I also talked to Chris, privately, for about five minutes and started crying. I told him that my family group session is tonight, and that I'm nervous about it. I told him some of the things that are bothering me.*

I like talking to him. It makes me feel better and worse at the same time. Pat and Chris help me feel the pain that I need to feel. It's good for me to feel because I usually keep everything inside.

March 8, 1991
It was good that I had another rehab to compare this one to. It makes me appreciate the stuff we can do here—like go outside and to off-grounds meetings. I think it's easier on my parents, too, to see me in my own clothes.

    I'm missing my senior prom tonight and I can't believe it. I know that I could've stayed clean there. I have a month sober today, the longest I've gone without alcohol since I was seven.

    We had a community meeting tonight and I shared about my issues. I talked about how I want to get the most out of my time here, and how I don't want to go to aftercare or partial. I guess it was good that I just participated. The meeting went on for two hours. This place isn't bad, it's actually kind of cool.

    Normally inpatients go into a partial program when they leave. They go to school and group at Wakeman and have family therapy. Twice a week they're there from eight-thirty in the morning to eight at night. After the partial program, they go into day school, going to their regular high school or Wakeman, and attending Wakeman for group.

    There was no way I was going to do either partial or day school. I wanted to return to Foran immediately. I wanted to leave Wakeman behind me. My favorite NA meetings were on Mondays and Thursdays. I'd have to miss them if I was in partial. Also, since I was going to college in the fall, I didn't want to graduate from Wakeman.

March 9, 1991
I have the shittiest chore there is on the weekend. We eat six times upstairs and I have to clean the kitchen after every meal. I got my 30 day CA keychain at the meeting this morning. We had a pretty cool day, I guess. Doing the kitchen sucks. We went to a stupid Disney movie today.

I talked to Ralph for a while in the office about suicide, cocaine, and things. I get to call my parents tomorrow. I can't believe there's only eight days left here tomorrow. Ralph goes, "Nine or more." I said, "Nope, no more than eight."

March 10, 1991
Andrea just told me that I have to write an essay called "Who Is Chris?"

I'm going to try to get into the habit of praying in the morning. That way I'll be doing it when I get home.

I finally got to call my parents. It was not good news. The Milford Citizen *interview ran today, and the story they printed wasn't very cool. My story was the first sentence in the article. It's a complete disaster. My parents and grandparents are seriously hurt. My parents want to kill Chris Burke for arranging the interview. I cannot believe this shit happened. This could hurt me in a big way. I begged to talk to Chris and they couldn't get in touch with him. So Emma called Dave Cornelio (the director) and he's gonna bring in the article tomorrow. And Chris is probably going to come in, too. This is one of the worst things that has ever happened to me. We called a group meeting and talked about it. I was freaking out. Before I hung up with my mother, I told her to call my grandparents and tell them it was all a misunderstanding. I hope they aren't as hurt as I imagine they are.*

Reaching Out to Kids in Crisis
Group deals openly with drug abuse

(Editor's note: Some of the names in this story are real, and some are not. Some students are so proud of their efforts to overcome drug and alcohol abuse that they want to use their real names. Some students have been abused or come from alcoholic families and do not want their names used.)

Chris was high on cocaine last year when she and a friend slashed tires at Lauralton Hall.

Two weeks ago, she went back to her former school and apologized, telling them the act was directly related to the drug and alcohol problem she has had since she was 7 years old.

Chris is one of the students at Joseph A. Foran High School and Jonathan Law who attends weekly group meetings at school with Chris Burke, coordinator of community programs for the Children's Center, a drug and alcohol rehabilitation facility in Hamden

"I started drinking when I was 7," Chris tells the 15 students in the room on this day. "I would stay with my grandparents every weekend. My grandfather is an alcoholic, and I stole beer out of the refrigerator."

"I found out I liked it," she says simply. "My dad is an alcoholic, too, so when I got home, I just kept on."

Chris graduated to pot at age 10, to coke and speed at 13. She stole from her grandparents, parents, friends' parents and sold gifts.

"My life has been so unmanageable the past few years," Chris says. "I was lying so much to everyone, I just felt like killing myself. I started going to Alcoholics Anonymous with my Dad."

The students nod when they hear she is going back to rehab. Then they applaud.

The article goes on, but that was the only part about me.

March 11, 1991
Chris better come down here today. I don't know why they had to make the article so identifiable that my grandfather could recognize me immediately.
Everyone in Milford knows about me now. This is too much. My father and my grandfather are never going to forgive me. I wish I knew why it is that every time my life starts going well something bad happens to screw me over again.

Today is a month clean. The longest I've had in years. The other day was a month without drinking. Somehow it isn't making me as happy as I thought it would. I can't stop thinking about the article. It makes me feel sick. At least I'll be in Arizona in five months and I won't have to deal with these things. They'll probably have forgotten about the article for the most part when I leave here, though. Family therapy should be interesting tomorrow. My mom wants Chris to be there. I still can't believe the whole town knows about me. How many tire slashers are there who got kicked out of Lauralton last year?

I talked to Chris and that made a big difference. I started crying, which I personally think he enjoyed. He said it's not my fault and I have to stop beating myself up over this stuff. He said to stop blaming people and accept that I'm powerless over my family and everyone else. He said he would be pissed if I let this bring down all the good shit I've been doing.

Emma almost gave me a consequence for swearing, but she hasn't put it on the board yet. Of course it was after Chris told her it was a miracle that I haven't gotten one yet.

March 12, 1991
I have the bathroom as my chore now. I hope my mother has calmed down some for family therapy today. It'll blow over with time. I'll apologize to my grandfather when I get home. Betsy says the treatment team thinks I should stay a couple of extra days. I said no way. I don't care if they like it or not, the deal was 14 days. I would stay longer if I wanted to.

Jeff and I sprayed the fire extinguisher in the school building hall by accident, so a meeting was called and lunch was an hour and 15 minutes late. The entire community of inpatient, partial, and aftercare was bitched at. We missed a cigarette break.

Family session went very well. My parents still want to meet Chris, but that's okay. I'm definitely going home on Monday and back to school on Tuesday. I'll try to do my best for the time that remains here. I talked to Ralph again today, he's so cool. I also talked to Gary and he's the only one who seems to think I'll do well when I leave here. I talked in the community meeting about my defenses and keeping people away from me, like how I have no trouble talking to people who don't really know me, but when it comes to someone who knows me well, I just can't put how I feel into words.

March 13, 1991
Thank God I'm leaving Monday, but things are going great, despite that article. Tonight I'll ask Ralph if he's got any words of wisdom for me. He's going on

vacation, and I may not see him again for a while. I shared at the CA meeting. We got two new residents and now there are 14 people inpatient. It's crazy. They'll be glad I'm gone Monday. I talked to Ralph for a few minutes, and we discussed my leaving. I have to say good-bye to him when I'm done writing this. He said they have a good gut feeling about me, which makes me feel better. I'm kind of going to miss this place, but I'll come to visit. I love life now. And I feel so good about myself. I never thought it could be this great. I never want to use again.

I sent Jill a letter. I want our friendship to stay the same. She means too much to me to lose it. When I get home, I hope all my friends still want to hang around with me. I'm a little anxious about that. I'm sure nothing has changed. All I have to worry about is today. Whatever happens, happens.

March 14, 1991
I saw Pat today, and I actually got to sit down and talk to him for a couple minutes. He came up to the unit and we sat in the office. I thanked him for what he's done for me, and he said that's nice, but if I want to thank someone it should be the kids in the group and Dave Ullman. He said he'll stop by and visit the group at Foran sometime. I'm lucky to have all these people in my life. I've been having chest pains all day and it reminds me of cocaine. I had my last session with Betsy this morning. We wrote out my post-treatment contract. It's much like the Arms Acres one I did. I miss Pat a lot. He was the first person I ever felt completely comfortable talking to about my drug use. Parent visiting was tonight and I had a nice visit

with my mother. I feel good about going home. Jill called my mother yesterday to see how I'm doing. I'm glad; that makes me feel a lot better. Ralph came by today, and I talked to him for a while. Gary reconfirmed with me that I do have a feel for the program.

March 15, 1991
We just had a group that took up most of rest period because two kids got level drops. It was so great to finally get all my aggressions out. We were yelling and swearing. I haven't had that much fun in a long time. I thought I was going to jump up out of my chair and hit someone. I think I really scared a couple of people. It was the first time I've gotten so excited in a long time. Pam, a counselor, said to me at the end, "Well, I'm glad we finally got to see the other side of you, Chris." And I said, "Hell yeah, this is me, tire slasher, angry, the whole bit. I can't take much more of this."

I probably wouldn't have talked at all in the group if I wasn't going home Monday. But hell, I don't have anything to lose. This is the most therapeutic group we've had yet!

Our community meeting went well. It was tense. Before it started I stuck up for Sue, and Laura, a counselor, said, "I'm sick of hearing your mouth, Chris." She told me I'm never going to stay clean because I have a bad attitude. I told her in the meeting that it pisses me off when she says stuff like that. It was cool. I got some more aggressions out. Some of us were having fun afterward talking about it. We couldn't watch TV or listen to the radio, nothing. Not even play cards. I'm surprised I didn't get a consequence today.

We had suspended privileges for the weekend because of group. Anything we did depended upon our behavior. Therefore, we didn't do much. The staff all kind of had an attitude on Saturday because of group the night before. It was extremely hard for me to get and keep a positive attitude.

March 16, 1991
I'm waiting to clean the bathroom. There are so many girls on the unit, it's a bitch to clean. I'm gonna appreciate all the things I took for granted when I get home. I had a great day today. I played basketball with Jeff, Mike, and Brad. It felt good to exert some physical activity. We all talked a lot since we have no privileges.

March 17, 1991
Thank God I'm finally going home tomorrow. I can't wait. I can't believe I have less than 36 hours left in this place. I'll never have to be in a place like this again. I know I can do it now. I never felt homesick once; I really don't miss being home at all. I just miss my freedom. It's a completely different situation going to college. I'll be able to do whatever I want out there. School's going to drag by tomorrow. I can't wait to be back at Foran on Tuesday and see everyone.

I had a good call to my mother. At least there were no more newspaper articles.

We went bowling this afternoon. I've never been a big fan of bowling, but it was fun. I finally got a consequence for swearing at Jamie. Harold gave it to

> me. I told Jamie to fuck himself, and I did it three more times after Harold warned me, so he finally gave me a consequence. I have to write a 350 word essay on "Why I must understand why swearing is not allowed at Wakeman Hall." This place was a great experience for me. I'm glad I came.

I ended up doing two essays for Andrea and Harold called "Who is Chris?" The first one they didn't accept because it was too nice. This is the second:

Who Is Chris?

I am a person who hides behind masks. I try to hide my real feelings because I am afraid of hurting others. I'm a "people pleaser." I like to make people happy. When people fight it makes me nervous, and then I'm the "peacemaker." I have lied, cheated, and stolen. Before I truly took on the people-pleasing role I didn't care who I hurt. I was cruel to my classmates and family. I fought with people physically and verbally. I played malicious pranks, like breaking car windows, etc. I wanted acceptance, and I got it by making other people's lives miserable.

    I hated my childhood. I looked forward to the day I could start drinking or doing drugs. I resented my father for not paying enough attention to me. As I got older I hated him for it. There are many resentments that I hold. I resent my mother for "poisoning" my mind against my father. I didn't like it when she told me he hated me or they never wanted a kid, or that I ruined their lives. When my parents told me things like that, I felt unlovable. When I started getting into trouble, I didn't like the way they paid attention to me. I felt it was too little too late, and I just wanted to be left alone. I still like to isolate myself sometimes.

When I did cocaine I hurt many people I didn't mean to. That left me with so much guilt. Two people who meant a lot to me have never been the same to me since I sent them a letter while I was high. I slashed the tires of a person I like just because I didn't want to back down on my friend. (I held a lot of guilt inside after that, but recently I made amends to her, and now I feel a great deal better.) When it came to choosing between cocaine and a friend, I would always pick cocaine.

If I don't get my way about something I will manipulate until I can get it. I don't do this as much as I once did, and not in serious situations. But I still have the capacity to do it. At one time I may have been described as vengeful, morbid, apathetic, volatile, etc. I felt as if my life was hopeless and pointless.

For the past two years I have been leading a double life. On one side I was an overachiever, honors student, leader in school and community—the kind of person no one would suspect of having a problem with drugs or alcohol. Then I would become a loud, obnoxious person who had no respect for anyone, including myself. I would have done anything for drugs, no matter who I was hurting. I could be two different people with no problem, depending on who I was talking to. One day I would be begging for help because of drugs, and the next I would be denying I had a problem at all.

I am a confused person. In one respect I have

> my whole future planned out. But at the same time I am unsure of what my future will actually hold. I'm not proud of the things I did in my past, but I can't dwell on that. Every day I'm changing, and I really am not the same person I was about 45 days ago. There's a lot of pain in my life still, but now I have ways of dealing with it in a healthy manner. Now I don't have to keep all my fear, anger, and frustration bottled up inside. I have people to talk to. I feel really lucky today to be alive and dealing with this disease. I understand that I will never make it if I don't get totally honest with myself. But just for today I am happier than I ever have been before. I know I'm not a scumbag or a loser.

They liked this paper better, but I still got the impression that it wasn't exactly what they had in mind. I didn't have the energy to delve into my soul and pull out every deep, dark secret I had. I tried my best to portray who I am. I guess it's hard for me to put together both pictures of who I think I am. I believe that I did honestly lead two separate lives. It was almost as if I had two personalities.

> *March 18, 1991*
> *I'm leaving today and I'm real excited about it. In about eight hours my mom will be here to get me. I have to write Harold's swearing consequence during school. I already have my stuff put out on my bed. I'm ready to go, all I have to do is pack. I've got to give everyone my address and phone number. In a way I don't want to leave, but in more ways I want to go home!*

In group that afternoon we had a little fun with the therapist. We told her that Jack's name was Frank and she believed it. She called him Frank for the whole hour. We loved it. Every time someone would speak we would all be oversupportive and thank them for five minutes for sharing with us. Then we told the therapist that Kevin had been in juvenile hall and was kicked out eventually for slicing up another kid with a knife he made in metal shop. We had the best time. Later on there was a group for me to say good-bye and thank everyone personally for what they did for me. It was an interesting afternoon. Harold gave me a medallion and said he had a good feeling I was going to make it.

My mother came a bit early, and I was still packing my stuff and talking to Andrea. When I was ready, I went over to the unit to say good-bye to everyone. I gave Marie a meditation book she had liked. They were in group, so I said good-bye to Harold, who was running it. Ralph was in Dave's office and I talked to them for a couple of minutes and then said good-bye. Andrea went with me to meet my mother. I said good-bye to Andrea and we left. It was sad; I didn't want to go. In a way, I actually wished I could stay.

CHAPTER TEN
▼

My first day back at school went well. It was great to be back. It started off with my mother and me going to see Mr. Kosh, the vice-principal, about the *Citizen* article. My mother was still angry. She told him that our family was extremely disappointed. They discussed it for a few minutes and I felt pretty stupid sitting there. Mr. Kosh told her that the school had helped me a great deal, and that the article was not meant to hurt anyone. It was supposed to give the public an idea of what the groups and the Student Assistance Team were doing for the kids in the high schools. I went down later to talk to him after my mother left. I explained to him what our problem was with the whole thing. He was understanding about our position on it.

My teachers were all very understanding about where I'd been and were willing to give me time to get back into things. I felt great. I was doing better than I'd had in years. I knew that I didn't have to keep up any defensive walls anymore. I could be myself.

I couldn't believe how much life had improved. My family was being very supportive and my parents were taking an active part in my recovery. Every night I would tell them which meeting I was going to, and we'd talk about meeting topics and the program. The three of us had dinner together often. We were communicating. Things were falling right into place. Instead of feeling like a failure, I felt my life was just beginning. I could think of nothing else to ask for.

On March 21 I had 40 days clean. During school I talked to Mr. Kosh and he had a lot of nice things to say to me. He made it clear that they were pleased with where I was at. I was grateful that they realized how much help they'd been, and still were, to me. He said that I helped them, too. I felt like I was living proof that the Student Assistance Team worked. He said that I was able to help myself more than most people because of my ability to verbalize. I agreed with him that it was worth it to get the article printed if even one person got something out of it. He told me that it was great to see me getting my life together.

Things went well until my first Friday, the beginning of my first weekend out of Wakeman. My compulsion to use began during group, which lasted about an hour and a half. I asked Chris to come talk to me later during my time with Dave. I was really thinking about using. I wanted a drink so badly I could taste it. Before I saw him I went outside to have a cigarette. I was almost shaking because I was so afraid of drinking that night. When I got up to the room, Chris told me that it was natural for me to feel that way after recently leaving treatment. He said I probably should have stayed longer at Wakeman instead of going right back to school at Foran. He had me talk out what my nights and weekends would be like if I picked up a drink. After we talked I sat in Mr. Kosh's office for about 20 minutes, and he got Rachel out of class to talk with me. Rachel and I sat in the group room talking about my desire to use. When it was time for her to go to class I felt better, and by the time I drove home the compulsion had passed.

I still believed that I'd made the right decision going back to Foran instead of going into partial. I concluded that Chris was always right about me, though, and that pissed me off. I felt like he could read my mind. I wasn't comfortable with people understanding me so well. It had been my need to control my life that led me to returning to Foran immediately. I wasn't going to say anything about my urge to drink, but I knew if I kept it in I would end up drinking. I needed to see the consequences I'd face if I drank. Not the least of which on my list was my pride. I would feel like a failure if I drank. So I told both Chris and Mr. Kosh that I wanted to get shitfaced drunk that night. I thought I might as well let them know that I didn't want one beer, I wanted a keg. I wanted to get trashed. I did the right thing that night by going to a meeting and sharing about what had happened. When it was all over I felt like things had really changed for me. I was going to stay clean and sober.

Everything was great until the *Citizen* ran an editorial responding to the first article. The editorial wasn't nearly as bad as the first one, but I was almost as angry as I was the first time. It still bothered me because it once again reminded my friends' parents of what I had been involved with, and it reminded my family as well. The school was pleased with the articles. I went to school the next day ready to kill someone, preferably a teacher on the Student Assistance Team or an administrator. It didn't help the way I felt when I walked into Mr. Kosh's office and saw the article posted on the outside of his door.

March 28, 1991
I talked to Chris Burke about the article, and I guess it was good for me to hear what he had to say. He told

> *me to stop feeling sorry for myself. He said that I'm feeding into negativity and looking for an excuse to get high. He said I'm setting myself up for relapse. And what bothers me was that he was right on all counts. I told Chris that it wasn't fair that other people could use and I can't. He said you're right, life isn't fair, too bad. He backed that up by saying, "For once you're doing what you need to do and not what you want to do." I have to stop feeling sorry for myself, otherwise I'll never change.*
>
> *I can't believe I'm going to be 18. I'll never be perfect, but I'll also never be the person I used to be.*

When things start to go well for me I often get nervous. I don't know how to handle positive activity. I'm used to a great deal of insanity, and when I'm not in trouble or busy I don't know how to react. I feed into negativity because I feel comfortable that way. If something upsets me, I will allow myself to dwell on the negative effects it has on me. In a way it seems as though I enjoy my anger and hostility. I jump at the chance to vent my emotions at people. Chris Burke once told me that he doesn't believe that I can talk to him without my lashing out at him for the first few minutes of our conversation. He is right; it is a defense for me to include sarcasm and hostility in the beginning of a discussion in which I may allow myself to be vulnerable. I thrive on insanity. I work well under pressure. The more things that I have myself involved in, the better I do. That goes for school especially. If I have many responsibilities, I tend to succeed more than when I am bored. I also enjoy finding ways to fight with people, not everyone, but some people.

The night before my 18th birthday, I had a vivid drug dream about cocaine. I woke up with a bloody nose and chest pains. But the next day I had a great birthday. We had a family party. No one said anything about the *Citizen* article, but they did seem to be acting strangely toward me. It was the first sober birthday I'd had in a long time.

I felt that this birthday was one in many chapters closing in my life. The first thing was getting clean. The next would be graduation. Things were changing for the better. But I was afraid of what the future was going to bring me. I was overwhelmed by the thought that I could never drink or use drugs again for the rest of my life. It seemed impossible. I had to learn to live a day at a time.

> *April 1, 1991*
> *There was a bloodmobile at Foran today. I spent periods 3 through 6 trying to give blood. Then I was talking to one of my friends and he convinced me that I should check "yes" on the form asking if I ever did drugs intravenously. I didn't want to because no one knew that I'd done it. They wouldn't take my blood. I got indefinitely deferred from giving blood.*
>
> *For some reason I had a real desire to shoot heroin today. It was so strange. I've never had that urge so strongly before. I wanted to drink, too, but that's no surprise.*
>
> *I had an interesting conversation with my mother a few minutes ago. I told her about the bloodmobile and how I used to shoot cocaine. I told her I have no control over my use, and that's what makes me an addict and an alcoholic. I think it's hard for her to realize that about me, that the problems I have are because of my addictive personality. I take risks without thinking. She says I have no common sense. Well maybe that's part of it. I like to live dangerously,*

on the edge. We both agreed that I have no respect for my own life, or death. Things are different for me now though. I don't want to die. I don't have that "fuck it" attitude anymore. My use of chemicals left me completely out of control.

April 2 , 1991
I can see so many great things in my future. I leave for Arizona State University in four months. I'm so glad I didn't die. I have too much to lose. God means so much to me now. Not that I'm religious or anything. It's nice to have something to believe in. All the time that I was determined to keep spirituality out of my life I was practically killing myself.

I had absolutely no cravings or desires to use today.

April 5, 1991
We had a two-hour group with Chris Burke today. It was pretty interesting. Chris read everybody the letter I sent him. I brought up that I've been getting urges to shoot heroin lately, and Chris enlightened me on that. He said that it's my disease progressing without me doing a thing. I don't know if I've used enough to progress to that already. It's scary if it's true.

Greg thinks that I'm depressed. I was a little defensive with him because it was the first time in years that I don't agree with that. I'm just feeling so good that I don't see it in myself. Maybe I'm in denial, but I doubt it. Chris liked his letter. He said he doesn't get many, or hasn't in his six years at Wakeman.

April 10, 1991
Sixty days clean. I had a great day today. I registered as a Republican. I also put down a deposit to buy a 20-gauge shotgun. I have to wait two weeks before I can get it. I have a clean record. I can't believe I'm finally going to get a gun of my own. This time I'm doing it to shoot skeet, not myself.

April 13, 1991
I called NA in Phoenix today and asked the lady who answered to send me a schedule of meetings. But I don't know if they will or not. The lady said they advise people to go to a meeting and pick one up. So I told her that would be pretty difficult since I live in Connecticut. Hopefully they'll send me one.

I was cleaning out the drawer in the table next to my bed tonight, and I found an empty coke vial and some cut straws. I thought that I had done a pretty good job of throwing everything out. Apparently not. I threw them out, along with an Elavil bottle full of .22 bullets left over from my suicide days. There were empty Corona six-pack cartons in my closet. I threw them all out but one. It's hard to part with things from my using past.

In school I was trying hard not to glorify the things that had happened to me when I was high. I kept remembering the stupid things I did when I was baked, usually when I smoked pot along with doing other drugs. One day when we were about 14 years old, I was at the beach in West Haven with Tricia. We often smoked pot in public with no concern for who might see us. We walked out onto a pier and got stoned. I had cotton mouth. The wind was blowing pretty hard. By accident,

I spit in her face. She didn't think it was as funny as I did.

Another time, while Chuck and Tricia and I were sitting in my backyard, I was pulling up grass and yelling, "Grass! I want to smoke some grass!" I thought it was the funniest thing I ever heard. It was probably the same day I was setting fires in the backyard and putting them out with the garden hose.

Back then, when I was using, I used to feel like I was not in reality, but rather that I was living in a dream. At one point I was diagnosed as having depersonalization disorder, which is when someone shifts in and out of reality. When this was happening, I'd first start perceiving things as getting darker. Then a light aura surrounded people and objects. I often felt as though I were not a real person but an observer in another person's life. I believed I could not survive without drugs. I thought that the way I was living was normal. Using drugs was a way of life. I said that people who criticized me were just jealous because they wanted to use, too. When something was bothering me, I'd lie to myself to make it seem like it wasn't related to anything I was doing.

For years I was using while in total denial that I might have a drug problem. Even when my problems occurred directly because of my drugs, I denied it. I thought I was in complete control of my situation. I manipulated people in order to keep using. I was living my own idea of what life should be like. I knew the risks of using, but I ignored them by believing that they couldn't apply to me. I could handle my problems by myself. When I needed help, I asked people around me, but they couldn't do anything. I needed to do it myself.

Finally, when it was impossible to change the situation, I asked a higher power for help. Then I'd get angry. I'd say there was no God because I didn't get what I wanted. Now I know who I can go to for help. I live in reality now. It may be hard sometimes, but it feels a lot better than before.

April 22, 1991
A lot of shit happened today and I feel kind of overwhelmed. I spent an hour with Kris, Cindy H., and Julie during second and third periods. Kris relapsed on crack last weekend. Julie's mother doesn't think she needs to go to treatment. Cindy either wants to run away or kill herself. I called Pat and talked to him about aftercare. I talked to Chris Burke briefly, too. But the four of us got a lot out of talking to Mr. Dodd. We explained to him what was going on, and we worked out what they should do next. Cindy came to my Spanish class as a visitor, because I didn't want to leave her alone.

April 24, 1991
Mark came to school with me for today, and I asked Dave if he had called that reporter from the Citizen *yet. He said yes, but we don't think that you're ready to see her yet. That pissed me off. He went on to imply that I never finished an inpatient program. Then he said what everyone likes to say to me—let's see what Chris Burke has to say about you talking to the* Citizen *reporter. Well, I really don't care what Chris has to say. I called Pat again today. He was gonna talk to his boss this morning to see if it's okay for me to go to aftercare at Branford Wakeman.*

Pat thanked me for the letter I sent him and asked if it would be okay for him to read it to the kids in the Branford program. I guess he wants to show them that the program works. I've come a long way since September.

April 25, 1991
It looks like I won't be allowed to work at the hospital anymore. I don't think they allow addicts to volunteer. They know about me because when I went to Arms Acres my mother called the director of Volunteer Services and said that I was going to be in rehab for a month. I'm going to the hospital Wednesday at 2:00 to talk about whether or not I can continue there.

April 26, 1991
I told Dave about my not being able to volunteer anymore and he was upset, but I'm okay with it. I feel strange about it though. I've been there for a year and a half. I should be able to stay. I was doing it while I was active, they should want me there even more now. He wants me to have Chris write them a letter, but I don't think that's necessary. I need to do things for myself. I need to prove that I'm worthy of the trust of the hospital on my own.

April 30, 1991
I'm officially not volunteering anymore. But that's okay. The director pissed me off though. She was treating me like I'm a low-life and I hate hat. Asking me stupid questions, personal things that I'm not obligated to tell anyone. It really aggravated me.

The whole thing with the hospital was pretty screwed up. I could accept that I couldn't volunteer until I had a year clean. But it was hard for me when I thought about how I wasn't using anymore. I guess I was a security risk, especially since part of my job working in the emergency room was making pharmacy trips. But the way that the director was talking to me bothered me a lot. She was asking me what my drug of choice was. I was not comfortable with that at all. I'm not sure why. I guess it was because I wasn't used to them thinking of me in that way.

May 10, 1991
Ninety days clean! I haven't done cocaine in 100 days. I had a great day. I wrote a letter to the group, thanking them and saying how I never thought that I'd have 90 days clean. Chris kept it. I guess he liked it.

May 14, 1991
Mr. Dodd and Mrs. Draz (my algebra teacher from junior year) both had good things to say to me today, about how well I'm doing. She said, isn't it amazing what you can do when there are no chemicals in your mind?

May 20, 1991
I had an interesting day. Mr. Dodd told me that my letter to the group was shared with the faculty. He said,"You wrote that letter Chris Burke read at the faculty meeting, didn't you?" Then he said Chris and some of the faculty almost started crying when he read it. Chris said hearing something like that makes his job worthwhile. Mr. Kosh also told me again that he is impressed with my progress. My gratitude to Foran is overwhelming. There are only 15 days of school left. That's it, the end of high school. On to bigger and better things.

On May 22, a freshman at Foran died after being struck on the head with a baseball. It was a serious tragedy. During a practice for the varsity, JV, and freshmen teams, Scott was serving as the cutoff man. The assistant coach hit a line drive by accident and Scott was struck in the temple.

May 22, 1991
Scott died today. He'd been comatose and in critical condition ever since being hit Monday. I can't believe that poor kid died because of a baseball. Things like that shouldn't have to happen. I feel so bad for his family, his teammates, and the coaching staff. The whole school has been affected by this, including those who didn't know him. The school did a lot to support everyone. They had a counselor come from Milford Mental Health, and held special meetings with the teammates. I hope God has a reason for taking this kid's life.

May 23, 1991
I can't help but think about how unfair it was that Scott died. There were so many times that I wanted to die, and I couldn't even when I tried. This kid was playing the sport he loved one minute and was fatally injured the next. Where is the justice in this world?

I had mixed feelings about June 6 because it was the day that Lauralton had graduation. In one way, I felt bad because I couldn't graduate with my original high school friends. In another way, I was very grateful for leaving the school and was happy to be alive to see the graduation. As it turned out, I couldn't go to the actual ceremony. I went to a reception they had at the school after the ceremony.

June 6, 1991
I went to the reception and said good-bye to everybody. It was kind of sad. It hit me that I may never see most of them again, because I won't be invited to reunions or anything. I was in a very good mood when I left. School went well today. Tomorrow is skip day. I'm picking up Jen Kelly so we can go out to breakfast first. Then we'll go to the last group of the year. Today Mr. Dodd said, "Chris, you've done a lot for your friends. When you bring someone down to talk to me, I listen because I know it must be important." That's cool. I've brought quite a few people down to talk to him about things. I'm leaving Foran with a good reputation.

Our last group was June 7. I was under the impression that we would continue having group over the summer, so it didn't hit me that that was it. Not many people showed up for group, but that was okay. I got the addresses of everyone who was there, so I could write them from Arizona. It was sad. I knew I was going to miss everyone, including Chris Burke.

It was also senior skip day, so right after group I drove Kathy and some other kids to a beach party in Bridgeport. There were six kegs. It was the first time in my sobriety that I exposed myself to a large amount of alcohol. It was fun for the first couple of hours. I was one of the few people not drinking. Then a brawl broke out. As soon as it settled down, we left.

On June 10 one of my good friends wrote me a very touching letter. She was one of the people who have helped me so much. I don't think I could ever let them know how much gratitude I have for them.

> Dear Chris,
> I feel you are the best example of someone who really wants to succeed. When I first met you in September of 1990, I thought, she will be dead in a short time. But as months went on, hope grew stronger. You all of a sudden changed for the better. I can't tell you how proud I am of you. Here you are now, clean, and on your way to college. I wish you all the luck in the world. I've never known anyone like you, Chris.
> Sincerely,
> Jen Kelly

I was overwhelmed by that. During the months prior to that, I had looked to Jen and the others in group for help all the time, whether it was between classes, outside while smoking, during class time, anytime. They were always there for me. Once I was clean, whenever they came to me for help I did my best to come through for them as well.

I was a bit anxious about the end of high school. I was nervous about going out to Arizona. But I made the most of my last few days at Foran. I had really loved going to that school. It was great. My favorite time of the school day was hanging outside during lunch in the parking lot, smoking with my friends. On nice days it could be a great time. On rainy days we stood under the overhang of the doors leading outside. It wasn't "legal" to smoke during the school day, but who really cared? If we wanted a cigarette, we would smoke one. I managed to go through four years of high school without getting one detention. Of course, I got kicked out of a school, so I guess that made up for all the detentions I didn't get. I also enjoyed skipping classes on nice days to sit outside. Since New England weather is very unpredictable, we cherished those days. I think I skipped more classes after I got clean than I did when I was using. I never got caught though.

> *June 12, 1991*
> *I have mixed emotions about today. I guess I'm both happy and sad. I've been waiting for years for graduation and now I don't want it. I got my yearbook today. I saw Burke, and he signed it, "Get a life and keep it." I said good-bye to Dave, and it hit me when I left that that was it. No more Physics, no more hellish AP English, no more Spanish with Don, Mike, and Armpit. And thank God, no more Algebra II! One more chapter in my life has closed. No more group on Friday. It's over. I had a great time this year. I'm going to miss everything about it. I made so many excellent friends. I failed Soviet History for the final grade. He lost the paper I wrote on Tchaikovsky. It was so good, too. Oh well. Who would've thought I'd make it and be so happy?*
>
> *Mr. Dodd came to class today with the letter I gave Mr. Kosh. He was so happy. I'm so glad that everything worked out so well. The letter was basically thanking Kosh and the Student Assistance Team. I'm their success story of the year. I hope they never forget me. I'd like to thank Lauralton again for kicking me out. It was the biggest favor anyone ever did for me. It's too bad that I didn't spend all four years at Foran.*

On June 13 we had class night. It went really well. I had worried about it for about a month because I didn't want to wear a dress, and all the other girls were. But then I said to myself, I don't care if the other girls are wearing dresses. I'll wear what

I want, and they'll like it! I wore pants and went with Mike from work. It was really cool. I never felt so accepted by my peers. I had a great time. We all signed yearbooks and just reminisced. For a minute I actually considered going out to the parking lot and drinking with my friends. But as I looked at them, I knew I couldn't. Just to confirm that I shouldn't drink, I went over to Joe and Jen, from group, and told them I was considering drinking. They threatened my life.

June 14, 1991
We got our caps and gowns today. While I was working on my book tonight, I stumbled across a letter that my mother wrote to me the first night I went to Arms Acres. I never saw it before. It was in the back of one of my notebooks. I almost started crying twice. I decided to write a letter to Mr. Kosh and share it with him. I never want to use again. What my mom wrote is very powerful. I think that Kosh can get something out of it. Maybe even a better understanding of just how grateful I am to them.
This is the letter my mother wrote :

February 9, 1991
Christiane,
Here is a letter for you to read, so that you can understand how much your father and I love you and care about you.

Tonight when I got home my brother Kris called before I got a chance to tell your father about our day, so he listened to me tell Kris. Then Bonni called and he listened again. Then he said to just get off the phone so that he could talk with me.

So then he said that he thought that it was all a

mistake to send you to Arms Acres and that he would just stay home with you 24 hours a day and help you, but that we had to go get you tomorrow (Sunday). I said you shouldn't be treated like a criminal, because you are a good person and you just need some help, not to be punished.

And anyway, now it's 10:40, and I'm thinking, okay light's out, she's probably really tired and trying to fall asleep because she has to get up at 7:00 A.M. And then I'm thinking about the past few years, and in about five minutes I think of four times that I found coke vials or glassine envelopes, and I thought you took them from someone to look cool for your friends or something.

Now I'm starting to realize why the parents are the last ones to know their child has a problem with drugs. Because we love you, and so we believe you the first time you deny something. I also probably didn't want to even think about you possibly *wanting* to do coke. You're so young, and it's dangerous. Your friends and family need you here, well again, soon I hope.

For now I think I can get your dad to wait until our Monday appointment at Arms Acres. They are forcing us to each list four to five statements that we have to read out loud to you and then they aren't going to let us talk to you. They wouldn't let me tell you that we have this appointment. That's why I said, "We'll see you soon." Your father said tonight that he has made a mistake, that he's going to start talking with you. That would be great.

The house seems very empty without you.

I thought that it was a very touching letter. It made me feel like abstaining from drugs for the rest of my life. I could feel the pain again, of letting down myself and my family. But I realized that I didn't have to feel that way anymore, because I am always changing. There is no standing still for me anymore.

June 15, 1991
I have no problem accepting that my life today is a miracle. Nothing is going to make me lose what I have today. I've never had it this good—Burke was right when he said that.

June 18, 1991
Kathy and I went to see Mr. Kosh after graduation practice and I gave him my mother's letter. For a minute I think he started crying. It was a nice moment. I guess he was really touched by it. Then he signed my yearbook. He's such a nice guy. We were just sitting there in his office and I shared a very personal letter with him. It's my way of showing my appreciation to him, and my trust as well. Today was very special for me; things have turned out so well.

June 19, 1991
I have 131 days clean. I'm a high school graduate. I can't believe that this was it. These past four years have flown by. The ceremony went very well. It rained, so it was inside, but it was still great. My grandparents went with my parents, and I snuck Al in. I wanted him to be there. Rachel and Kathy showed up. Tonight we went to a party, and it was cool. I said good-bye to some of my friends, in case I don't see

them before I leave for school. My mother went up to Mr. Kosh after the ceremony and thanked him for all he's done for me. That was nice. It doesn't really feel like I've graduated. They even spelled Christiane right on my diploma. I got a C for the year in Algebra. My life is so good, what more could I ask for?

Most people don't know what it is like to feel lucky to be alive for graduation. On my graduation day I knew that I almost didn't make it. I was fully aware of how fortunate I was to be there. One more chapter in my life was closing, one of many chapters that had been closed that year. I was a new person with a different outlook on life. When I walked down the aisle and received my diploma, I knew I would never touch another drug as long as I lived. There was too much to lose.

AFTERWORD
▼

January 1993

No Guarantees was not written to glorify drugs or alcohol. I am not proud of many things that I have done. I have led a rather bizarre life compared to most people, and have done some harsh things to my body. It has done nothing but damage me in the long run. I now have a heart condition that forced me to take a medical withdrawal from my first semester at college. It is very scary for me because sometimes my heart races so fast that I feel like I'm going to pass out. When I was doing cocaine I felt the same way, and now that I am in recovery I don't want to feel that way.

I am a student at Arizona State University and consider myself very lucky to be there. In fact, I consider myself very fortunate to be alive. This book ends with my graduation from high school. At that point I had changed considerably since becoming clean and sober. I graduated almost 18 months ago now and I am still changing. I have over 23 months clean and thank God for every day that I remain so.

To say that the changes in my life have been dramatic would be an understatement. I am a very different person now. Today I feel healthy; I have control over my life and the direction it takes. I am happy and I have friends who respect and like me for who I really am. This is not to say that my life is perfect and everything is always great, because it's not.

Although I don't think about drugs often, college is a

place where alcohol and drug use is everywhere. When my friends sit back and drink beer I do feel envy toward them. Sometimes I wish I was normal and could control my drinking, but I cannot. I have the disease of addiction and am not able to control my use. There is no such thing as social drinking for me, and I am certainly not capable of what some people call "recreational" drug use. If I choose to drink a beer, or smoke a joint, or snort a line of cocaine, I might as well sign my own death certificate. I take everything to extremes.

My recovery is everything to me today. It has become a way of life. I have choices today and I choose to continue to grow and become a better person. I no longer feel that I am at a standstill. Things are always changing, for better and for worse. However, I can deal with the obstacles that life throws at me, and I know that there are other addicts out there, just like me, whom I can count on. Today they can count on me as well. I have spirituality and balance in my life now, and that has helped to fill the void in me that I tried so hard to fill with drugs and alcohol.

Despite the pain my life-style caused me, and although I did things I am ashamed of, I would not change one thing from my past. Everything I did, all the lessons I've learned, have made me the person I am today. I am comfortable with myself, I have a family whom I love and who love me, I have friends that I wouldn't trade for anything, I have self-respect. Drugs never gave me any of that. I realize that there are no guarantees that I will stay clean and sober. I could go out tomorrow and get high, or I could get hit by a bus. No one can tell what will happen. All I can do is think about the present and stay clean a day at a time. If I need to be reminded what it was like to get high, I can just read my book. That would make me think twice about using.

GLOSSARY
▼

acid: LSD
baked: intoxicated on marijuana, stoned
basing: freebasing (smoking) cocaine
blow: cocaine
bone: a marijuana cigarette
bowl: a marijuana pipe
bud: a small clump of the marijuana plant
crash: the low point, coming down from a high, such as one caused by cocaine
crystal meth: methamphetamine; a stimulant
deadhead: a Grateful Dead fan
detox: clearing system of drugs and alcohol, first step of most treatment centers
dug out: an enclosed marijuana pipe
eightball: 3.5 grams of cocaine
grinder: cocaine paraphernalia
head shop: a store that sells drug paraphernalia and items such as incense
hit: one dose of LSD, or other drug
joint: a marijuana cigarette
jonesin': craving
LSD: a hallucinogenic drug
mainline: inject intravenously
major stoner: someone who smokes marijuana regularly

ripped: drunk
speed: amphetamines, stimulants
Student Assistance Team: A group of faculty members who monitor and intervene in high-risk students' lives.
trashed: drunk
trip: LSD intoxication
Vivarin: an over-the-counter stimulant
wired: high